EPHESIANS

Together in Christ

Group Directory

Pass this Directory around and have your Group Members
fill in their names and phone numbers

Name   **Phone**

_____   _____

_____   _____

_____   _____

_____   _____

_____   _____

_____   _____

_____   _____

_____   _____

_____   _____

_____   _____

_____   _____

_____   _____

_____   _____

_____   _____

EPHESIANS

Together in Christ

EDITING AND PRODUCTION TEAM:
James F. Couch, Jr., Lyman Coleman, Sharon Penington, Cathy Tardif,
Christopher Werner, Matthew Lockhart, Mary Chatfield, Scott Lee,
Erika Tiepel, Richard Peace, Andrew Sloan, Gregory C. Benoit

NASHVILLE, TENNESSEE

Together in Christ: A Study of Teamwork Based on Ephesians
© 1988, 1998, 2003 Serendipity House
Third reprint 2009

Published by Serendipity House Publishers
Nashville, Tennessee

ISBN: 978-1-5749-4322-7
Item No. 001197652

Dewey Decimal Classification: 227.5
Subject Headings:
BIBLE. N.T. EPHESIANS-STUDY AND TEACHING \ CHRISTIAN LIFE

Scripture quotations are taken from the Holman Christian Standard Bible®,
Copyright © 1999, 2000, 2002, 2003 by Holman Bible Publishers.
Used by permission.

To purchase additional copies of this resource or other studies:
ORDER ONLINE at www.SerendipityHouse.com
WRITE Serendipity House, One LifeWay Plaza, Nashville, TN 37234
FAX (615) 277-8181
PHONE (800) 525-9563

1-800-525-9563
www.SerendipityHouse.com

Printed in the United States of America

Table of Contents

Core Values

Community:
The purpose of this curriculum is to build community within the body of believers around Jesus Christ.

Group Process:
To build community, the curriculum must be designed to take a group through a step-by-step process of sharing your story with one another.

Interactive Bible Study:
To share your "story," the approach to Scripture in the curriculum needs to be open-ended and right brain—to "level the playing field" and encourage everyone to share.

Developmental Stages:
To provide a healthy program throughout the four stages of the life cycle of a group, the curriculum needs to offer courses on three levels of commitment: (1) Beginner Level—low-level entry, high structure, to level the playing field; (2) Growth Level—deeper Bible study, flexible structure, to encourage group accountability; (3) Discipleship Level—in-depth Bible study, open structure, to move the group into high gear.

Target Audiences:
To build community throughout the culture of the church, the curriculum needs to be flexible, adaptable and transferable into the structure of the average church.

Mission:
To expand the Kingdom of God one person at a time by filling the "empty chair." (We add an extra chair to each group session to remind us of our mission.)

Introduction

Each healthy small group will move through various stages as it matures.

Growth Stage: Here the group begins to care for one another as it learns to apply what they learn through Bible study, worship and prayer.

Develop Stage: The inductive Bible study deepens while the group members discover and develop gifts and skills. The group explores ways to invite their neighbors and coworkers to group meetings.

Birth Stage: This is the time in which group members form relationships and begin to develop community. The group will spend more time in ice-breaker exercises, relational Bible study and covenant building.

Multiply Stage: The group begins the multiplication process. Members pray about their involvement in new groups. The "new" groups begin the life cycle again with the Birth Stage.

Subgrouping: If you have nine or more people at a meeting, Serendipity recommends you divide into subgroups of 3–6 for the Bible study. Ask one person to be the leader of each subgroup and to follow the directions for the Bible study. After 30 minutes, the Group Leader will call "time" and ask all subgroups to come together for the Caring Time.

Each group meeting should include all parts of the "three-part agenda."

 Ice-Breaker: Fun, history-giving questions are designed to warm the group and to build understanding about the other group members. You can choose to use all of the Ice-Breaker questions, especially if there is a new group member that will need help in feeling comfortable with the group.

 Bible Study: The heart of each meeting is the reading and examination of the Bible. The questions are open, discover questions that lead to further inquiry. Reference notes are provided to give everyone a "level playing field." The emphasis is on understanding what the Bible says and applying the truth to real life. The questions for each session build. There is always at least one "going deeper" question provided. You should always leave time for the last of the "questions for interaction." Should you choose, you can use the optional "going deeper" question to satisfy the desire for the challenging questions in groups that have been together for a while.

 Caring Time: All study should point us to actions. Each session ends with prayer and direction in caring for the needs of the group members. You can choose between several questions. You should always pray for the "empty chair." Who do you know that could fill that void in your group?

Sharing Your Story: These sessions are designed for members to share a little of their personal lives each time. Through a number of special techniques each member is encouraged to move from low risk, less personal sharing to higher risk responses. This helps develop the sense of community and facilitates caregiving.

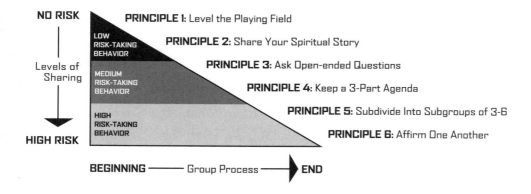

Group Covenant: A group covenant is a "contract" that spells out your expectations and the ground rules for your group. It's very important that your group discuss these issues—preferably as part of the first session.

GROUND RULES:

- Priority: While you are in the group, you give the group meeting priority.

- Participation: Everyone participates and no one dominates.

- Respect: Everyone is given the right to their own opinion and all questions are encouraged and respected.

- Confidentiality: Anything that is said in the meeting is never repeated outside the meeting.

- Empty Chair: The group stays open to new people at every meeting.

- Support: Permission is given to call upon each other in time of need—even in the middle of the night.

- Advice Giving: Unsolicited advice is not allowed.

- Mission: We agree to do everything in our power to start a new group as our mission.

ISSUES:

- The time and place this group is going to meet is_____

- Refreshments are _____ responsibility.

- Child care is _____ responsibility.

Other great resources from Serendipity House...

MORE

More depth, more meaning, more life.

Discovering truth through Bible study is much more than breaking a verse down to its smallest part and deconstructing a passage word by word. There is context and experience, mystery and story that all go into fully understanding the Word of God. By dissecting down to the smallest part, we often lose the essence of the whole. For this reason, Serendipity introduces a new approach to the inductive Bible-study format that looks at each passage within the context of the larger story. This reunifies the cognitive aspect with an experiential dynamic and allows the truths of scripture to come alive in new and unexpected ways.

Song of Songs: The Epic Romance | 1574943405
Job: A Messy Faith | 1574943464

Mark: Beyond the Red Letters | 1574943413
Colossians: Embrace the Mystery | 1574944150

GOD AND THE ARTS

Where faith intersects life.

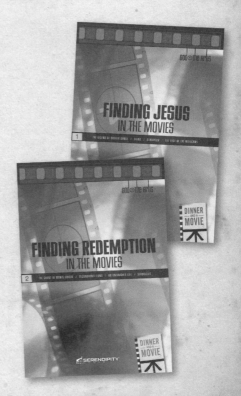

Stories, great and small, share the same essential structure because every story we tell borrows its power from a Larger Story. What we sense stirring within is a heart that is made for a place in the Larger Story. It is no accident that great movies include a hero, a villain, a betrayal, a battle to fight, a romance, and a beauty to rescue. It is The Epic story and it is truer than anything we know. Adventure awaits. Listen.

Discover an experience that guides you on a journey into the one great Epic in which the Bible is set. These fun and provocative studies features four films, each with two small-group meetings, _Dinner and a Movie_ (Week 1), _Connecting the Dots_ (Week 2), and an _Experience Guide_ that offers valuable insights.

Finding Jesus in the Movies | 1574943553
Finding Redemption in the Movies | 1574943421

Spiritual Blessings

Scripture Ephesians 1:1–14

The book moves from theory to practice; from doctrine to duty; from what God has done to what we are to do. The emphasis throughout Ephesians is on unity. In chapters 1–3, Paul extols the great reconciling work of Christ, who through his sacrificial death overcame the demonic powers and thus broke down the wall between God and man and the wall between Jew and Gentile. Then, in chapters 4–6, Paul exhorts us to live out this unity through a series of imperatives. The city of Ephesus was the capital of the Roman province of Asia. It was a large, bustling, secular city situated on the west coast of Asia Minor on the Aegean Sea. Originally a Greek colony, by Roman times it had become a center for international trade, largely as a result of its fine, natural harbor.

Paul's first visit to Ephesus was brief—little more than a reconnaissance trip (Acts 18:18–22). He later returned during his third missionary journey and spent over two years there. His ministry was effective and controversial. After three months in the synagogue, he was forced out and took up residence in the lecture hall of Tyrannus (Acts 19:8–9). Paul probably worked as a tentmaker in the mornings and lecturer in the afternoons. News of his message spread throughout Asia Minor (Acts 19:10). Extraordinary things happened. Handkerchiefs touched by him were used to cure the sick (Acts 19:11–12). Demons were cast out by the name of Jesus, even by Jewish exorcists (Acts 19:13–17). Pagan converts burned their books of magic arts (Acts 19:18–20). Eventually, a riot broke out in Ephesus because of Paul. Demetrius, a silversmith, organized a citywide protest. He charged that Paul's success posed a threat to the economic well being of craftsmen who made their living from the worshipers of Artemis (Acts 19:23–41). As a result, Paul moved on to Macedonia. But by this time the church was firmly established.

Paul never visited Ephesus again. He did, however, stop at the nearby port of Miletus on his return to Jerusalem. He called the elders of the Ephesian church to him there and gave a moving farewell address (Acts 20:13–38). Later on, Paul would write 1 and 2 Timothy in an attempt to deal with false teaching that had arisen in Ephesus—as he had warned in his farewell address might hap-

> *Welcome to this study of Ephesians. Paul's letter to the Christians living in Ephesus is one of four letters known as the Prison Epistles, written while Paul was in jail. It is written to neighboring churches in the Roman province of Asia, which is modern-day Turkey. Paul most likely wrote this letter around A.D. 60, some 30 years after Jesus' resurrection and a few years before Paul's death.*

pen (Acts 20:28–31). His words and Timothy's ministry were apparently successful. The book of Revelation records that the Ephesians resisted false teaching—though they had lost their first love (Rev. 2:1–7). Tradition has it that John the apostle spent the final years of his life in Ephesus—as the beloved bishop and last surviving apostle.

Ice-Breaker Connect With Your Group (15 minutes)

Today we are beginning our journey through Ephesians with a look at the many blessings we have as children of God. Take turns sharing with one another some thoughts and experiences about blessings and family.

1. When you "count your blessings," what are the top three items on your list?

2. What is something in your family that you would like to inherit someday?

3. Growing up, was there something that you felt destined or "chosen" to become?

Leader
Be sure to read the introductory material in the front of this book prior to this first session. To help your group members get acquainted, have each person introduce him or herself and then take turns answering one or two of the Ice-Breaker questions. If time allows, you may want to discuss all three questions.

Bible Study Read Scripture and Discuss (30 minutes)

Paul opens his epistle by introducing to his readers a great "mystery" (v. 9), that sinners who were once far away from God can now be more than reconciled: we can even be adopted into the family of God. Read Ephesians 1:1–14 and note the glorious inheritance we have in Christ.

Spiritual Blessings

Leader
Select a member of the group ahead of time to read aloud the Scripture passage. Then discuss the Questions for Interaction, dividing into subgroups of three to six. Be sure to save time at the end for the Caring Time.

1 Paul, an apostle of Christ Jesus by God's will:
   To the saints and believers in Christ Jesus at Ephesus.
²Grace to you and peace from God our Father and the Lord Jesus Christ.
³Blessed be the God and Father of our Lord Jesus Christ, who has blessed us with every spiritual blessing in the heavens, in Christ; ⁴for He chose us in Him, before the foundation of the world, to be holy and blameless in His sight. In love ⁵He predestined us to be adopted through Jesus Christ for Himself, according to His favor and will, ⁶to the praise of His glorious grace that He favored us with in the Beloved.

[7]In Him we have redemption through His blood, the forgiveness of our trespasses, according to the riches of His grace [8]that He lavished on us with all wisdom and understanding. [9]He made known to us the mystery of His will, according to His good pleasure that He planned in Him [10]for the administration of the days of fulfillment—to bring everything together in the Messiah, both things in heaven and things on earth in Him.

[11]In Him we were also made His inheritance, predestined according to the purpose of the One who works out everything in agreement with the decision of His will, [12]so that we who had already put our hope in the Messiah might bring praise to His glory.

[13]In Him you also, when you heard the word of truth, the gospel of your salvation—in Him when you believed—were sealed with the promised Holy Spirit. [14]He is the down payment of our inheritance, for the redemption of the possession, to the praise of His glory.

Ephesians 1:1–14

Questions for Interaction

Leader
Refer to the Summary and Study Notes at the end of this session as needed. If 30 minutes is not enough time to answer all the following questions, conclude this section by skipping to question 7.

1. Do you know anyone who is adopted? How has adoption affected that person?

2. What does it mean to be "adopted through Jesus Christ" (v. 5)? How does this change a person's life?

3. In this passage, what "mystery" has God revealed as part of his ultimate plan and purpose (see note on v. 9)?

4. What does it mean that a believer is "sealed with the promised Holy Spirit" (v. 13)? What purpose does this serve?

5. What are the spiritual blessings in Christ found in this passage? Which of these blessings is most meaningful to you?

6. When did you come to the place in your spiritual journey that you fully understood what God did for you in Jesus Christ?

7. Where do you stand in relation to God right now?

   ○ Close.
   ○ Off again, on again.
   ○ Challenged.
   ○ I'm not sure.
   ○ Distant.
   ○ Other _____.

8. What does it mean to be "holy and blameless" in God's sight (v. 4)? How does a person attain this? How does it affect his or her life?

Caring Time Apply the Lesson and Pray for One
Another **(15 minutes)**

As we begin our study together as a group, our goal will be to support one another in the things we are learning and the struggles that we are facing. Spend some time now sharing your life and praying with one another.

1. Agree on the group covenant and ground rules that are described in the introduction to this book.

2. Recall the blessings mentioned in today's Scripture passage. What would you like to thank God for today?

3. Share any other prayer requests and praise items, then close in prayer. Pray specifically for God to lead you to someone who can join you next week to fill the empty chair.

Leader
Take some extra time in this first session to go over the introductory material at the front of this book. At the close, pass around your books and have everyone sign the Group Directory, also found in the front of this book.

NEXT WEEK *Today we considered what it means to be adopted into God's family. We were reminded of the many wonderful blessings we have as followers of Christ. In the coming week, reflect each day on how you, as an adopted child of God, can best be like your Father in heaven. Next week we will learn about the power and majesty of God.*

Summary: Paul begins with a long blessing (1:3–14) and then follows this with an equally long thanksgiving (1:15–23). The blessing (which will be studied here) is, in Greek, a single, complex sentence that just seems to tumble from Paul's lips. So intent is Paul on praising the work of God in the lives of Christians that he simply heaps phrase upon phrase. However, roughly speaking, in verses 3–6 his focus is on the past election by God the Father. In verses 7–12 he shifts to the present redemptive activity by Jesus Christ the Son, while in verses 13–14 his concern is with the future inheritance guaranteed by the Holy Spirit.

1:1 *apostle.* Apostles are much like ambassadors. They are chosen by the king (in this case Jesus) to represent him and are given power to act in his name. This was the title that was given the original Twelve (Luke 6:13) and then later to Paul (Gal. 1:11–24). By using this title, Paul indicates that he is writing with the authority of Jesus Christ.

1:2 *Grace to you and peace.* This is the undeserved favor of God freely given as a gift. "Peace" refers to the reconciliation of sinners to God and others. Taken together they define the central theme of Ephesians: peace through grace.

1:3 *Blessed.* This whole paragraph is a hymn of praise to God. Paul "blesses" God for his work of grace. The verb "praise" can also be translated "to speak well of" and carries the idea of thanking, glorifying and singing the praises of the one who is the object of this gratitude. *God.* God is the subject of virtually every main verb in this passage. At those places where the verbs are passive (vv. 11,13), it is the work of God that is being described. It is God's work of love, grace and redemption that generates all this praise. *Jesus Christ.* It is in and through Jesus that God's work of love, grace and redemption is performed. In the first 14 verses Jesus is named or referred to some 15 times. Eleven times the phrase "in Christ" or "in him" is used. *has blessed us.* The tense of the Greek verb indicates that what is in view here is a single, past action on God's part. *spiritual blessing.* This

phrase may mean that the blessing God gave was spiritual, in contrast to the Old Testament stress on material blessing. However, the phrase "spiritual blessing" could also mean "every blessing of the Holy Spirit." In this case (from Paul's first words), the work of the Trinity is seen—God the Father, God the Son and God the Holy Spirit. *in the heavens.* This is a phrase used by Paul only in Ephesians, where it occurs five times (1:3,20; 2:6; 3:10; 6:12). It refers to the unseen world of spiritual reality.

1:4 *holy and blameless.* In 5:27 and Colossians 1:22, this phrase is used to define the goal of the Christian life: people who have been made perfect and whole. (The Greek word translated here as "blameless" is used to describe the kind of animal that was acceptable as an offering to God—one that was perfect and without blemish.)

1:5 *predestined.* Literally, "marked out beforehand." Predestination is a difficult but thoroughly biblical doctrine, characteristic of God's activity in the Old Testament in choosing Israel (Ex. 19:4–6; Deut. 7:6–11; Isa. 42:1), and in the New Testament in choosing the church, which is the new Israel. *adopted.* This was a common Roman (but not Jewish) custom, in which a child was given all the rights of the adoptive family by grace, not by merit (or birth). *His favor and will.* This phrase carries with it the sense that God goes about such choosing with great joy. This is not the arbitrary action of an impersonal potentate ...

1:7 *redemption.* Setting someone free (originally prisoners or slaves) by payment of a ransom (in this case, Jesus' death in place of the sinner). *forgiveness of our trespasses.* The child of God is not only given freedom from the penalty of sin, but the sin itself is forgotten. Redemption and forgiveness go together.

1:9 *mystery.* The word focuses on the disclosure of what was once hidden but is now revealed by God. In this case, the astonishing fact is that the final goal of history is for this hopelessly divided world (Jews against Gentiles, male against female, etc.) to be united under Christ.

1:10 *to bring everything together.* From a Greek word meaning "to sum up," as in the conclusion of a speech or a column of figures; a gathering together of the pieces into a whole.

1:11–13 *In Him we … In Him you.* Jewish Christians who first believed (we) are now joined by Gentile believers (you), a clear sign that traditional barriers are crumbling.

1:13 *sealed.* A mark placed by an owner on a package, a cow or even a slave. The cults in the first century sometimes tattooed a mark on their devotees. *promised Holy Spirit.* This is the second of three terms in verses 13–14 used to describe the Holy Spirit. The Spirit is not only "promised," but the "seal" whereby the Christian is marked out as belonging to God and the "down payment" (v. 14) of that Christian's future inheritance. The Holy Spirit was promised in the Old Testament (Ezek. 36:27; Joel 2:28) and by Jesus (Luke 24:49; John 14–16; Acts 1:4–5; 2:33,38–39; Gal. 3:14).

Thanksgiving and Prayer

Scripture Ephesians 1:15–23

> **LAST WEEK** *In last week's session, Paul reminded us that we are adopted children of God, sealed into his inheritance by the Holy Spirit. We also saw the many blessings that we have as followers of Christ, including "redemption through His blood" and "the forgiveness of our trespasses" (1:7). This week we will focus on the power and majesty of God.*

 Ice-Breaker Connect With Your Group (15 minutes)

Paul opens his letter with a prayer, thanking God for his friends and reflecting on the majestic power and glory of Jesus Christ. Paul is proud to be associated with Jesus. Take turns sharing the thoughts and experiences you have had with thankfulness and admiration.

Leader
Begin the session with a word of prayer. Have your group members take turns sharing their responses to one, two or all three of the Ice-Breaker questions. Be sure that everyone gets a chance to participate.

1. When it comes to writing thank you notes, which are you?

   ○ Novelist.
   ○ Short story writer.
   ○ Procrastinator.
   ○ Right on time.
   ○ Other _____.

2. Growing up, who was your favorite superhero, and why?

   ○ Spider Man.
   ○ Super Man.
   ○ Bat Man.
   ○ Bionic Woman.
   ○ Mighty Mouse.
   ○ Other _____.

3. What "title" have you had applied to you that pleased you the most?

Bible Study Read Scripture and Discuss (30 minutes)

Leader
Ask two members of the group, selected ahead of time, to read aloud the Scripture passage. Then discuss the Questions for Interaction, dividing into subgroups of three to six.

Paul continues his epistle by praying for his audience, asking God that they may come to see the great riches that the Lord wants his people to inherit. Read Ephesians 1:15–23 and note how Paul emphasizes the power and glory of God.

Thanksgiving and Prayer

Reader One: [15]This is why, since I heard about your faith in the Lord Jesus and your love for all the saints, [16]I never stop giving thanks for you as I remember you in my prayers.

Reader Two: [17]I pray that the God of our Lord Jesus Christ, the glorious Father, would give you a spirit of wisdom and revelation in the knowledge of Him. [18]I pray that the eyes of your heart may be enlightened so you may know what is the hope of His calling, what are the glorious riches of His inheritance among the saints, [19]and what is the immeasurable greatness of His power to us who believe, according to the working of His vast strength.

Reader One: [20]He demonstrated this power in the Messiah by raising Him from the dead and seating Him at His right hand in the heavens— [21]far above every ruler and authority, power and dominion, and every title given, not only in this age but also in the one to come. [22]And He put everything under His feet and appointed Him as head over everything for the church, [23]which is His body, the fullness of the One who fills all things in every way.

Ephesians 1:15–23

Questions for Interaction

Leader
Refer to the Summary and Study Notes at the end of this session as needed. If 30 minutes is not enough time to answer all of the questions in this section, conclude the Bible Study by answering questions 6 and 7.

1. For whom do you pray regularly?

   ○ Parents.
   ○ Spouse.
   ○ Children.
   ○ Grandchildren.
   ○ Church.
   ○ Small Group.
   ○ Missionaries.
   ○ The President.
   ○ Friends.
   ○ Boss.
   ○ Enemy.
   ○ Other _____.

2. What was Paul's prayer for the people to whom he was writing (vv. 17–19)? What motivated his prayers?

3. Which of the things that Paul prayed for could you most use in your life right now?

4. What is one way that God has displayed his power in the past? Where do you see his power at work now?

5. What do we learn about Christ from verses 20 through 22?

6. What are you doing in your life to nurture the "spirit of wisdom and revelation in the knowledge of Him" (v. 17)?

   ○ Daily time with God.
   ○ Consistent prayer life.
   ○ Studying the Bible.
   ○ Being careful about thought life.
   ○ Submitting everything to God.
   ○ Other _____ .

7. Where in your life do you need the "immeasurable greatness of His power" (v. 19) to be at work in the coming week?

Going Deeper   If your group has time and/or wants a challenge, go on to this question.

8. What does it mean that Jesus is "far above every ruler and authority ... and every title given" (v. 21)? What implications does this have in today's world?

 **Caring Time** Apply the Lesson and Pray for One Another (15 minutes)

Too often we take for granted the love and friendship of the people around us. Today let's take the time to express our appreciation for the people who help us live godly lives.

1. What are you particularly thankful for this week?

Leader
Be sure to save at least 15 minutes for this important time. After sharing together from the following questions, share prayer requests and end in a time of group prayer.

2. What do you appreciate about this group?

  ○ Reality check.
  ○ Safe place to bring concerns.
  ○ Spiritual encouragement.
  ○ Honest friendships.
  ○ Prayer.
  ○ Bible Study.
  ○ Food.
  ○ Other _____.

3. Take time to thank God for some of the people who have been a blessing to you.

NEXT WEEK *This week we looked briefly at the power and majesty of God, and reflected on the people who have helped us to understand that. In the coming week, pray for others you know who need to see God's glory, and invite them to this group. Next week we will consider the power of God to give eternal life.*

Notes on Ephesians 1:15–23

Summary: Having praised the triune God for the incredible activity in, through and on behalf of his people (vv. 3–14), Paul now prays that the Christians to whom he writes will grasp the magnitude of all that has been done for them. "Enlightenment" is what he wants for them. He craves for them that they be able to "see" what is so (vv. 17–18). In particular, he wants them to grasp the hope to which they have been called; the glory of their inheritance and the magnitude of God's power. He ends this section focusing in particular on this last point, God's power.

1:15 *This is why.* The prayer that follows this phrase springs directly from the vision in verses 3–14 of the spiritual blessings given to us. *since I heard about.* Paul does not know the people to whom he writes. They may be Christians in Asia Minor, converted as the power of his ministry radiated outward from Ephesus (Acts 19:10); or they may be new Gentile Christians in Ephesus, converted after Paul left that region.

1:16 *thanks.* Paul's response to these new Christians is one of profound thankfulness. It is his thankfulness for this miracle of grace that compels him immediately to ask for enlightenment for them. He wants them to grasp the wonder of what has happened.

1:17 *wisdom and revelation.* Awareness of all these spiritual blessings will not necessarily come through logical dedication, nor solely as a result of experience. There must also be an inner work of God by which individuals are enabled to "see" and understand what is going on. *in the knowledge of Him.* Paul asks for two types of illumination. This is the first. He prays not that they will know about God, but that they will know him better.

1:18 *I pray that.* This is the second prayer for insight. Now he wants them to grasp three things in particular that flow out of this personal relationship with God. *the eyes of your heart.* The heart was understood to be not simply an organ that pumped blood. It was the very center of one's personality. Paul wants this illumination to strike right to the core of a person's being. *hope of His calling.* The mention of calling refers back to 1:4–5 and the idea of having been chosen to be holy and without blame, predestined to be adopted as God's sons and daughters. These phrases seem to define well the objective substance of this hope; i.e., they are God's children and they will be holy and not held accountable for their sins. *the glorious riches of His inheritance among the saints.* This is the second benefit derived from knowing God. The inheritance in mind here might refer to Christians as God's own inheritance or possession as they are often spoken of in the Old Testament (Deut. 32:9). More likely the idea is parallel to that in Colossians 1:12, and the reference is to the riches beyond imagination which God has reserved for his people (1 Peter 1:4).

1:19 *according to ... His vast strength.* Verse 19b reads literally, "the power is like the energy of the might of his strength." The first word is *dunamis* (from which "dynamite" is derived) or "power" and it denotes the ability to accomplish what is begun. The second word is *energeia* (from which "energy" is derived) or "working" and it means brute strength or muscle. The third word is *kratos* or "strength" and refers to the ability to face obstacles and overcome them. The final word is *ishus* or "mighty" and refers to the actu-

al use of power. Second, having said "God's power is like every conception you have ever had of power," Paul then points to three acts in history when that power was displayed. It was seen in the past in God's act of raising Christ from the dead. It is seen now in the present enthronement of Christ as King. It is also seen in the way Christ is head over the church.

1:20 *raising Him from the dead.* Jesus was really dead, buried in a tomb. But so mighty is God's power that it burst the bonds of death. Even centuries later, one can look back at that empty tomb (for which no adequate explanation apart from the Resurrection has ever been offered) and begin to grasp the extent and nature of God's power. *seating Him at His right hand.* Jesus is now the King who reigns in absolute power. One day that reign will result in the bringing together of all things under him (1:10; Heb. 2:5–9).

1:21 *ruler and authority, power and dominion, and every title given.* Paul wants to be quite clear that there is no power by any name—be it angelic or demonic, natural or supernatural, from the past or in the future—that stands outside the scope of Christ's powerful reign.

1:22 *under His feet.* Psalm 110:1, which was interpreted as a description of the absolute authority of the Messiah, may have been in Paul's mind.

1:23 *the fullness of the One who fills all things in every way.* Does this fullness refer to Christ (who is filled by God), or to the church? If the reference is to the church, in which sense: that the church "fills" or "completes" Christ, or that Christ "fills" the church? Each of these three interpretations is possible.

Made Alive in Christ

Scripture Ephesians 2:1–10

LAST WEEK *In our previous session, we examined the power and majesty of God, and gave thanks for the people in our lives who have shown us God's glory. We were also reminded that we should pray for wisdom and enlightenment so we may know the "hope of His calling" (1:18). This week we will discover more about God's limitless power: the power to raise the dead.*

 Ice-Breaker Connect With Your Group (15 minutes)

In today's passage, Paul will introduce us to the greatest gift anyone can ever hope for; yet he speaks of it while talking about death, an unexpected context. What gifts have changed your life? Have you ever been close to death? Take turns sharing your unique life experiences.

Leader
Open with a word of prayer, and then welcome and introduce any new people. Select from the Ice-Breaker questions to begin the study. Remember to stick closely to the three-part agenda and the time allowed for each segment.

1. What's the best gift you've ever received?

   ○ My first nice doll.
   ○ Favorite toy.
   ○ Pet.
   ○ A scholarship.
   ○ A pony.
   ○ When she said yes to marriage.
   ○ First Christmas bonus.
   ○ A trip.
   ○ Cash.
   ○ That first "A" in college.
   ○ Other _____.

2. What award or "merit badge" have you received in recognition of some good work?

3. What's the closest you've ever come to death? What saved you?

Bible Study Read Scripture and Discuss (30 minutes)

Leader
Ask two group members, selected ahead of time, to read aloud the Scripture passage. Then discuss the Questions for Interaction, dividing into subgroups of three to six.

In this section, Paul introduces the reader to another of the great "mysteries" of the Christian faith: that those who were once dead have been made alive again. This is the concept of regeneration through faith, a salvation that cannot be purchased by any work of man. Read Ephesians 2:1–10 and note the "immeasurable riches" of God's grace.

Made Alive in Christ

Reader One: 2 you were dead in your trespasses and sins [2]in which you previously walked according to this worldly age, according to the ruler of the atmospheric domain, the spirit now working in the disobedient. [3]We too all previously lived among them in our fleshly desires, carrying out the inclinations of our flesh and thoughts, and by nature we were children under wrath, as the others were also. [4]

Reader Two: But God, who is abundant in mercy, because of His great love that He had for us, [5]made us alive with the Messiah even though we were dead in trespasses. By grace you are saved! [6]He also raised us up with Him and seated us with Him in the heavens, in Christ Jesus, [7]so that in the coming ages He might display the immeasurable riches of His grace in His kindness to us in Christ Jesus.

Reader One: [8]For by grace you are saved through faith, and this is not from yourselves; it is God's gift— [9]not from works, so that no one can boast.

Reader Two: [10]For we are His creation—created in Christ Jesus for good works, which God prepared ahead of time so that we should walk in them.

Ephesians 2:1–10

Questions for Interaction

Leader
Refer to the Summary and Study Notes at the end of this session as needed. If 30 minutes is not enough time to answer all of the questions in this section, conclude the Bible Study by answering questions 6 and 7.

1. What time of day do you feel most alive?

   ○ Don't talk to me until after my morning coffee.
   ○ I'm ready to go at 6 a.m.
   ○ I'm pretty good between 10 and 10:30 in the mornings.
   ○ I don't fully wake up until noon.
   ○ I'm most creative in the evenings.
   ○ I start to really rock after midnight.
   ○ Other _____.

2. If we are "dead" because of sin (v. 1), how are we made alive?

3. According to verse 8, by what means does salvation come?

4. From this passage, what would you say to someone who wanted to know what to do to know Christ?

5. What is the relationship between God's grace and good works?

6. What has God's grace meant to you in your life?

7. How does it make you feel to know that God considers you his great masterpiece (v. 10)? What good work do you feel God may have in mind for you?

Going Deeper   If your group has time and/or wants a challenge, go on to this question.

8. If good works do not save people, what part do they play in salvation?

Caring Time Apply the Lesson and Pray for One Another (15 minutes)

Encouraging and supporting each other is especially vital if this group is to become all it can be. Take time now to share God's mercy and compassion and pray for one another.

1. Where are you in relation to salvation?

   ○ Curious.
   ○ I think I got it figured out.
   ○ Working on it.
   ○ Needing grace.
   ○ Really needing a lot of grace.
   ○ Fully alive.
   ○ Alive and growing.
   ○ Other _____.

2. Spiritually, do you feel more dead or alive right now, and why?

3. What do you appreciate about belonging to this group? How could you support one another in the coming week?

Leader
Be sure to save at least 15 minutes for this important time. After sharing together from the following questions, end in a time of group prayer. Remember to include a prayer for the empty chair when concluding the prayer time.

NEXT WEEK *Today we considered the fact that we all were once dead in our sins, and that God alone has the power to raise us to eternal life. In the coming week, if you have not been made "alive with the Messiah" (v. 5), ask God for the gift of eternal life that can only come from His grace. If you already have accepted the gift of eternal life, pray for someone who has not and invite him or her to this group. Next week we will learn that we can be more than just forgiven, we can become part of the family of God.*

Notes on Ephesians 2:1–10

Summary: Paul is emphasizing in this section that the ultimate reconciliation of all things in Christ Jesus, described in chapter one (1:9–10,20–22), is guaranteed by the reconciliation that has already been accomplished between God and people. In 2:11–22, he will further demonstrate this fact by pointing to the (unprecedented) reconciliation between Jew and Gentile, which likewise confirms that ultimate reconciliation will, indeed, occur. In 2:1–10, Paul describes this reconciliation between God and people by means of a series of triple contrasts. Whereas we were once enslaved to the world, the Devil and the flesh, now we have been made alive, raised up and seated with Christ.

2:1 *And you.* The "you" refers to the Gentiles in Asia Minor to whom Paul was writing. This is made clear in 2:11 where he says "you were Gentiles in the flesh." However, verses 1–3 are not just a portrait of decadent pagans. In verse 3a, Paul says "we too" lived the same way, thus including himself and his fellow Jews in this description. And in verse 3b he refers to "the others were also" indicating that the whole human race is like this. ***dead.*** They were spiritually dead; i.e., humanity in general is out of tune with God's ways and out of fellowship with God himself. Paul means this literally, not metaphorically. Without a relationship with God, people are dead within. ***trespasses and sins.*** These two words refer, respectively, to active wrongdoing ("sins of commission"), and passive failure ("sins of omission"). The image behind "transgressions" is of a person crossing a boundary fence into a forbidden field, or of a person wandering off the true path into the wrong way. The image behind "sins" is of an archer shooting arrows at a target, none of which hit the bulls eye. They all "fall short."

2:2 *walked.* This has the same sense of a deliberate choice of direction. The path one follows determines the way one lives in an ethical and moral sense. In contrast to following the ways of this world, Jesus calls people to follow him and his teaching. ***according to this worldly age.*** The idea of "this worldly age" refers to the fact that there would be two ages—this present evil age and a new, future age in which God would reign. "Worldly" refers to the system of values and perspectives around which society is organized and which is hostile to God. This is the first power to which people outside Christ are enslaved. ***ruler of the atmospheric domain.*** This is the first of several references in Ephesians to Satan. He is called "the Devil" in 4:27 and 6:11; and "the evil one" in 6:16. Here we learn that he is reigning monarch over a real kingdom, and that his kingdom is located in "the air" or "atmosphere." Furthermore, we learn that the Devil operates through spiritual means. The Devil is the second power to which people are enslaved. ***now working.*** Satan's activity is not only past, nor only in the future. It is here and now in this present evil age. *in the disobedient.* The main attribute of those who are "dead in ... trespasses and sins." They disobey God, who is the ultimate Ruler, and fail to live in accord with his way. They are, in fact, in active rebellion against him.

2:3 *our fleshly desires.* The word here is literally "the flesh," and it refers to self-centered human nature, which expresses itself in destructive activities of both body and mind. This is the third bondage under which humans struggle.

2:4 *abundant.* Paul makes more allusions to "riches" in Ephesians than anywhere else in his writings. *mercy.* Not only love, but mercy motivates God. The Greek word, *eleos,* is used in the Greek Old Testament to translate the Hebrew word *hesed,* which in English is "loving kindness" (KJV) or "steadfast love" (RSV). Love and mercy are not distant but closely related. *because of His great love.* Love is God's reason for rescuing fallen humanity (Deut. 7:6–9). This one of four words that Paul uses to explain God's motivation for reaching out to humanity. (The others are mercy, grace and kindness.)

2:5 *made us alive.* Paul coins this word to describe exactly what happens to us when we are "in Christ"; namely, we share in Christ's resurrection, ascension and enthronement. *By grace.* This resurrection from spiritual death cannot be earned. It is simply given. Grace is God's unmerited favor or gift to us. *you are saved.* The tense of this verb signifies a past action that has been completed. Paul is saying

that they "have been saved and remain saved forever." To be "saved" is how Paul describes being rescued or delivered from the triple peril of death, slavery and wrath.

2:7 *that in the coming ages He might display.* The change in life and status brought about in the Ephesians (and all who follow Christ) is another visible demonstration of the greatness of God's power. In this case, Paul says God displays "the immeasurable riches of His grace" by this work in humanity. *kindness.* Not only do love, mercy and grace describe God's character (and so explain his saving action on people's behalf), but Paul also adds kindness as the fourth element in this list of attributes.

2:8 *For by grace you are saved.* This is the second time Paul acclaims this amazing fact (v. 5). *through faith.* Salvation does not come about because of faith, salvation comes by grace through faith. The Greek word for faith, *pistis,* can also be translated "believing". Faith is believing, and includes a person's grateful response by which he or she accepts the gift of grace that has been offered.

2:8–9 *not from yourselves ... not from works.* Salvation is not a reward for what a person has done. It is not the result of being good or keeping the Law. Works stand in opposition to grace, which is the true origin of salvation.

2:10 *good works.* Although good works do not save a person, they do flow from that person as a result of salvation.

One in Christ

Scripture Ephesians 2:11–22

> **LAST WEEK** *In our last session, we discovered that, while mankind is dead in sin, God offers the power of resurrection through faith in Jesus Christ. We were reminded that love is the reason God has done this for us, along with his mercy, grace and kindness. This week we will focus on how Jesus came to break down all of the barriers that exist between people and keep them from loving one another.*

Ice-Breaker Connect With Your Group (15 minutes)

We all feel like we don't fit in from time to time. Share with one another some of the times when you have felt like an outsider or even an alien.

1. Where did your ancestors emigrate from?

   ○ Canada.
   ○ Central America.
   ○ South America.
   ○ Caribbean.
   ○ Asia.
   ○ Pacific Islands.
   ○ Middle East.
   ○ England.
   ○ Northern Europe.
   ○ Southern Europe.
   ○ Eastern Europe.
   ○ Africa.
   ○ Other _____.

Leader
Begin with a word of prayer, and then introduce any new people. Select one or all of the Ice-Breaker questions to get the group talking together.

2. Did you ever have to sneak into someplace because you didn't belong? What was it?

○ Party.
○ Club.
○ Sporting event.
○ Deserted house.
○ Other _____ .

3. When have you felt most like an alien or an outsider?

 Bible Study Read Scripture and Discuss (30 minutes)

Paul introduces the first of his themes of unity in this passage. Those of us who are not part of the Jewish race (Gentiles) were once cut off from access to God's presence. But now, through the blood of Christ, God has become available and accessible to the entire human race. Read Ephesians 2:11–22 and note how there are no strangers in God's family.

Leader
Ask two group members, selected ahead of time, to read aloud the Scripture passage. Have one person read verses 11–15; and the other read verses 16–22. Then discuss the Questions for Interaction, dividing into subgroups of three to six.

One in Christ

Reader One: [11]So then, remember that at one time you were Gentiles in the flesh—called "the uncircumcised" by those called "the circumcised," done by hand in the flesh. [12]At that time you were without the Messiah, excluded from the citizenship of Israel, and foreigners to the covenants of the promise, with no hope and without God in the world. [13]But now in Christ Jesus, you who were far away have been brought near by the blood of the Messiah. [14]For He is our peace, who made both groups one and tore down the dividing wall of hostility. In His flesh, [15]He did away with the law of the commandments in regulations, so that He might create in Himself one new man from the two, resulting in peace.

Reader Two: [16]He did this so that He might reconcile both to God in one body through the cross and put the hostility to death by it. [17]When Christ came, He proclaimed the good news of peace to you who were far away and peace to those who were near. [18]For through Him we both have access by one Spirit to the Father. [19]So then you are no longer foreigners and strangers, but fellow citizens with the saints, and members of God's household, [20]built on the foundation of the apostles and prophets, with Christ Jesus Himself as the cornerstone. [21]The whole building is being fitted together in Him and is growing into a holy sanctuary in the Lord, [22]in whom you also are being built together for God's dwelling in the Spirit.

Ephesians 2:11–22

Questions for Interaction

Leader
Refer to the Summary and Study Notes at the end of this session as needed. If 30 minutes is not enough time to answer all the questions in this section, conclude the Bible Study by answering question 7.

1. Who is someone that you admire as being a peacemaker?

   ○ Billy Graham.
   ○ Your mother.
   ○ Jimmy Carter.
   ○ Mother Teresa.
   ○ Wyatt Earp.
   ○ Other _____.

2. Before Jesus came, what problems did the Gentiles face (vv. 11–12)? What were the eternal implications of this for the Gentile world?

3. What does Paul mean by "the dividing wall of hostility" (v. 14)?

4. How has Jesus brought an end to this "hostility" and made peace possible for all people?

5. What does it mean to be "fellow citizens with the saints, and members of God's household" (v. 19)?

6. What "dividing wall" in our world would you most like to see come down?

7. What relationship in your own life has "walls" that need to be "torn down"?

Going Deeper If your group has time and/or wants a challenge, go on to this question.

8. If believers are "being built together" as part of God's sanctuary (vv. 21–22), how should that be reflected in your church? What could you do to help your church make people feel more welcome?

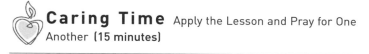

Caring Time Apply the Lesson and Pray for One Another (15 minutes)

Leader
Be sure to save at least 15 minutes for this important time. After sharing together from the following questions, end in a time of group prayer.

Encourage and pray for one another, keeping in mind that God is our Father and our source of peace (v. 14).

1. How would a person from a very different background feel when visiting this group? How can we work to reach out to and welcome such a person?

2. How can the group pray for you regarding your answer to question 7?

3. What do you need to change in your life in the coming week to live up to the calling of being a member of God's household?

NEXT WEEK *Today we considered how we were once apart from God with no hope for reconciliation. Through Jesus, however, we have more than just peace with God; we have become part of his family and part of his church. In the coming week, pray that the Lord will show you ways to break down walls between you and other people. Next week we will focus on the price that Paul paid to spread the Gospel to the Gentiles.*

Notes on Ephesians 2:11–22

Summary: Paul moves from the problem of human alienation from God (2:1–10) to the related problem of alienation between people themselves (2:11–22). In both cases, the problem is hostility (or enmity). Christ is the one who, through his death, brings peace—first between God and people, but then, also, between human enemies. The particular focus of this section is on the deep hostility between Jew and Gentile. Paul begins by reminding Gentiles of their fivefold alienation from God's plan for the world (vv. 11–12). But then he goes on to describe how Jesus' death overcame all that (vv. 13–18). Jesus abolished the Law that divided people from God and each other; he created a new humanity and he reconciled this new "race" to God. Paul concludes by describing, through three metaphors (kingdom, family, sanctuary), the new reality that has emerged (vv. 19–22).

2:11 *remember.* In 2:1–3, Paul reminded his Gentile readers that once they were trapped in their transgressions and sins, and so were spiritually dead and alienated from God. Here in verse 11, he asks them to remember that once they were also isolated from all the blessings of God. In 2:1–3, the focus is on being cut off from God himself; while in verses 11–13, the focus is on being cut off from God's kingdom and God's people. *"the uncircumcised."* This is a derogatory slur by which Gentiles were mocked. With this contemptuous nickname, Jews were saying that the Gentiles' lack of "God's mark" on their bodies put them absolutely outside of God's kingdom, so they were to be despised. *"the circumcised."* This is

how Jews thought of themselves, and was a term used with pride. Circumcision was the sign given to Abraham by which the covenant people were to be marked. This made the Jew different and special.

2:12 *without the Messiah.* In contrast to the great blessings that come as a result of being "in Christ," at one time the Gentiles were outside Christ. That is, they had no hope of a coming Messiah who would make all things right. Instead, they considered themselves to be caught up in the deadly cycle of history that led nowhere. The separation from the hope of a Messiah was the first liability faced by the Gentiles. *excluded from the citizenship.* Gentiles were not part of God's kingdom. Israel was a nation founded by God, consisting of his people, and Gentiles were outside that reality. This was their second liability. *foreigners to the covenants.* Not only did Gentiles have no part in God's kingdom, they also stood outside all the amazing agreements (covenants) God made with his people (Ex. 6:8; Deut. 28:9–14). This is the third liability. *with no hope.* During this particular historical era, the Roman world experienced a profound loss of hope. The first century was inundated with mystery cults, all promising salvation from this despair. Living in fear of demons, people felt themselves to be mere playthings of the capricious gods. This lack of hope in the face of fear was the fourth liability. *without God.* This is not to say that Gentiles were atheists (even though the word used here is *atheos*). On the contrary, they worshiped scores of deities. The problem was that they had no effective knowledge of the one true God. This is the final liability.

2:13 *But now.* This is the second great "But," which signals God's intervention into a seemingly hopeless situation. The first use of "But" in this fashion is found in 2:4, where Paul describes what God has done in the face of universal sin and bondage. *by the blood of the Messiah.* Paul pinpoints how this great change occurred. It is as a result of Jesus' death on the cross that union with Christ is possible (1:7).

2:14 *our peace.* Jesus brings peace; that is, he creates harmony between human beings and God. He also creates harmony between human beings. He draws together those who consider each other to be enemies. He does this by being the one who stands between the alienated parties, bridging the gap that separates them. *the dividing wall of hostility.* Paul may have had in mind an actual wall that existed in the temple in Jerusalem. The temple itself was built on an elevated area. The Court of the Priests surrounded the inner sanctuary. Beyond this was the Court

of Israel (for men only) and then the Court of the Women. All these courts were on the same level as the temple; and each had a different degree of exclusivity. Ringing all the courts and some 19 steps below was the Court of the Gentiles. Here Gentiles could gaze up at the temple. But they could not approach it. They were cut off by a stone wall ("the dividing wall"), bearing signs that warned in Greek and Latin that trespassing foreigners would be killed. Paul himself knew well this prohibition. He had nearly been lynched by a mob of Jews who were told he had taken a Gentile into the temple. *hostility.* The ancient world abounded in hostility. There was enmity between Jew and Gentile, Greek and barbarian, men and women, slave and free. Christ ends each form of hostility.

2:15 *the law of the commandments in regulations.* The primary reference is to the thousands of rules and regulations that were in existence at the time of Christ, by which Jewish leaders sought to define the "Law of Moses" (the first five books of the Old Testament). The belief was that only by keeping all these rules could one be counted "good," and therefore have fellowship with God. *one new man.* In the place of divided humanity, Jesus creates a whole new quality of being—a new humanity, as it were. This does not mean that Jews became Gentiles, or that Gentiles became Jews. Both became Christians, "the third race."

2:17 *He proclaimed the good news of peace.* Since such peace was possible only through the Cross, this reference is probably to Jesus' post-resurrection appearances. His first words to the stunned apostles after his resurrection were, in fact, "Peace be with you!" (John 20:19).

2:18 *access.* In Greek, one form of this word is used to describe an individual whose job it is to usher a person into the presence of the king. Indeed, not only did Jesus open the way back to

God (by his death, humanity was reconciled to God), he continues to provide the means whereby an ongoing and continuing relationship is possible.

2:19 *foreigners.* Nonresident aliens who were disliked by the native population and often held in suspicion. *strangers.* These are residents in a foreign land. They pay taxes, but have no legal standing and few rights. *fellow citizens.* Whereas once the Gentiles were "excluded from the citizenship of Israel" (v. 12), now they are members of God's kingdom. They now "belong." *members of God's household.* In fact, their relationship is far more intimate. They have become family.

2:20 *cornerstone.* That stone which rested firmly on the foundation and tied two walls together, giving each its correct alignment. The temple in Jerusalem had massive cornerstones (one was nearly 40 feet long). The image might be of Jesus holding together Jew and Gentile, Old Testament and New Testament.

2:21 *holy sanctuary.* The new temple is not like the old one, carved out of dead stone—beautiful, but forbidding and exclusive. Rather, it is alive all over the world, inclusive of all, and made up of the individuals in whom God dwells. *fitted together.* Used by a mason to describe how two stones were prepared so that they would bond tightly together.

Preacher to the Gentiles

Scripture Ephesians 3:1–13

> **LAST WEEK** *In our last session, we looked at how we were once cut off from God, separated from him and from others by walls of hostility, until Jesus brought us peace. We were reminded that Jesus breaks down all barriers and makes it possible for everyone to become part of God's household. This week we will learn how Paul's willingness to suffer for others actually brought "glory" to the Gentiles.*

Ice-Breaker Connect With Your Group (15 minutes)

Sometimes a secret ought to be told, because some things are too good to keep hidden. For example, if someone does something great for us, we should tell others about it. Take turns sharing your experiences with secrets and spreading good news to others.

Leader
Open with a word of prayer, and then introduce any new people or visitors. Select one, two or all three Ice-Breaker questions to begin the study.

1. Which phrase best describes how good you are at keeping a secret?

   ○ Mum's the word.
   ○ I know a secret, but I can't tell you.
   ○ I shouldn't say this, but ...
   ○ Quick, hand me the phone.

2. What is the best news that you've heard in recent months?

3. Did anyone ever do something for you that was very costly or painful for that person? What was it, and did you tell others about it?

Bible Study Read Scripture and Discuss (30 minutes)

Paul continues his explanation of the great mystery of reconciliation that has been made available to the Gentile world. God's grace has suddenly become available to all people, not just to the Jews. Read Ephesians 3:1–13 and note how Paul sees God working through his afflictions.

Leader
Select two group members ahead of time to read aloud the Scripture passage. Then discuss the Questions for Interaction, dividing into subgroups of three to six.

Preacher to the Gentiles

Reader One: 3 For this reason, I, Paul, the prisoner of Christ Jesus on behalf of you Gentiles— ^{2}you have heard, haven't you, about the administration of God's grace that He gave to me for you? ^{3}The mystery was made known to me by revelation, as I have briefly written above. ^{4}By reading this you are able to understand my insight about the mystery of the Messiah. ^{5}This was not made known to people in other generations as it is now revealed to His holy apostles and prophets by the Spirit: ^{6}the Gentiles are co-heirs, members of the same body, and partners of the promise in Christ Jesus through the gospel.

Reader Two: ^{7}I was made a servant of this gospel by the gift of God's grace that was given to me by the working of His power. ^{8}This grace was given to me—the least of all the saints!—to proclaim to the Gentiles the incalculable riches of the Messiah, ^{9}and to shed light for all about the administration of the mystery hidden for ages in God who created all things.

Reader One: ^{10}This is so that God's multi-faceted wisdom may now be made known through the church to the rulers and authorities in the heavens. ^{11}This is according to the purpose of the ages, which He made in the Messiah, Jesus our Lord, ^{12}in whom we have boldness, access, and confidence through faith in Him.

Reader Two: ^{13}So then I ask you not to be discouraged over my afflictions on your behalf, for they are your glory.

Ephesians 3:1–13

Leader
Refer to the Summary and Study Notes at the end of this session as needed. If 30 minutes is not enough time to answer all the questions in this section, conclude the Bible Study by answering question 7.

1. Like Paul preached to the Gentiles, who reached out to you and taught you the Gospel? Who actually led you to Jesus Christ?

2. What mystery that was made known to Paul is revealed in this passage? What mystery about the Christian faith are you still trying to understand?

   ○ That Jesus died on the cross for me.
   ○ That I am saved through grace, not by works.
   ○ That God can forgive my past.
   ○ That I can go to God in prayer about anything.
   ○ Other _____.

3. Consider the implications of the three metaphors that Paul uses to describe our relationship with God and with Israel in verse 6: co-heirs; members of the same body; partners of the promise. What do these things mean?

4. What was Paul's view of the mission God had given to him (vv. 7–10)?

5. How do Paul's afflictions bring about the "glory" of the Gentiles?

6. What wonderful benefit of being in Christ is mentioned in verse 12? On a scale of 1 (low) to 10 (high), with how much boldness and confidence do you approach God?

7. How would you compare Paul's passion to share the Gospel with your own?

Going Deeper   If your group has time and/or wants a challenge, go on to this question.

8. Explain what Paul means in verse 10, where he states that God's wisdom is now made known "through the church." How does it make you feel that you are part of God's plan and purpose that is so beautiful even "ruler and authorities" in the universe take notice?

 **Caring Time** Apply the Lesson and Pray for One
Another (15 minutes)

Leader
Encourage everyone
to participate in this
important time and be
sure that each group
member is receiving
prayer support.
Continue to pray for
the empty chair in the
closing group prayer.

The great news of salvation should never be kept a secret; it is the sort of spectacular news that should be spread abroad loud and clear. But sometimes doing so requires that the "news-bearers" pay a price. Gather around each other now in this time of sharing and prayer and give each other support and encouragement to go out and spread the Good News.

1. As you look ahead in your life what are you expecting?

   ❍ No problems on the horizon.
   ❍ I think that things are getting better.
   ❍ I have this feeling of dread.
   ❍ Things have got to change.
   ❍ It couldn't be worse.
   ❍ I'm afraid, because it's so good it has to go down hill from here.
   ❍ Other _____.

2. In what way might you be able to help carry the "affliction" of others to share the Gospel with them?

3. Whom do you know that you could reach out to with the Gospel and invite to this group?

NEXT WEEK *Today we considered how Paul's boldness and selflessness led to the Gentiles hearing of God's plan of salvation. In the coming week, consider prayerfully whether the Lord might be calling you to step out of your comfort zone and share his good news in some way that might be a bit costly. Next week we will focus on the power of prayer and the importance of love for others.*

Summary: This section is divided into two parts. First, Paul describes in verses 1–6 how he came to grasp the truth that Jew and Gentile are one in Christ (by revelation). Then, he explains in verses 7–13 how he came to preach this truth. Both his understanding of this mystery and his call to preach it are the result of "God's grace that was given to me." This phrase is used in verse 2 and in verse 7 by way of introduction to each theme.

3:1 *For this reason.* Paul mentions the Gentiles and it strikes him that he ought to say a word about how he came to be their apostle. He will pick up his prayer again in verse 14. *prisoner.* It is quite possible that Paul was under house arrest and not in a prison cell. He was probably in a rented home. He was able to read and write, and to receive visitors. However, he was chained day and night to one of a series of Roman soldiers. *the prisoner of Christ Jesus.* He was, in fact, Nero's prisoner. But Paul knows better. Nero may have the power to incarcerate him, but it is Jesus who commands his love, allegiance and freely given service. *on behalf of you Gentiles.* This statement is literally true. Paul was in prison awaiting trial precisely because of his ministry to the Gentiles. He was arrested in the first place because it was thought he had brought Gentiles into the temple in Jerusalem (Acts 21:27–32; 22:22–29). Throughout his ministry, his claim that God was creating a new people, who included Gentiles on an equal basis with Jews, aroused severe opposition. The vision he presented in chapter 2 is the cause of his suffering.

3:3 *mystery.* In English, this word has the sense of something that is hidden and perhaps even incomprehensible. In Greek, a mystery is something that is beyond human reason to figure out, but once God reveals it, it is open and plain to all. This is a key word in this passage. *revelation.* This new reality is not something Paul figured out on his own; nor was it the product of a theological committee. It was given by God.

3:4 *the mystery of the Messiah.* Paul has already explained in 1:9–10 the general nature of this mystery: that at the end of time all things will be united in Christ. But this new reality is not something to be realized only in the future. As he explains in verses 1–6, this mystery also has a here-and-now reality to it. The immediate meaning of the mystery is that Jew and Gentile have been made one in Christ.

3:5 *not made known to people in other generations.* In the Old Testament it was clear that the Gentiles would one day be blessed through Abraham (Gen. 12:1–3; Ps. 2:8; Isa. 2:2–4; 42:6–7; 49:6). In the New Testament, Jesus told his disciples to make disciples of all nations (Matt. 28:19). But what had not been made clear was the radical nature of God's intention—the union of both Jew and Gentile in Christ given concrete expression in a new body, the church. *revealed to His holy apostles and prophets.* It was not only to Paul that God revealed this new truth about the Gentiles. In Acts 10:9–23, for example, Peter learns by means of a divine vision that Gentiles are no longer to be considered impure and outside God's kingdom.

3:6 *co-heirs/members/partners.* Paul's point is that these two groups—once traditional enemies—now share together the same promised covenant blessings, the same body and the same benefits.

3:7 *servant.* In Greek, this word is *diakonos* from which the word "deacon" comes. It can also be translated "minister." Underlying both these ideas, however, is the concept of service. *this gospel.* The mystery revealed to Paul now becomes the message preached by Paul. *by the gift of God's grace.* In the same way that the mystery was revealed to Paul by grace (v. 2), so too his call to preach is by grace. *working of His power.* Here is another example of God's astonishing power. Paul, who killed Christians, has been transformed by that power into one who preaches Christ.

3:8 *the least.* Taking a superlative meaning "least" or "smallest" Paul alters, so that it becomes a comparative, meaning "leaster" or "less than the least." There is probably also some wordplay going on here. Paul's Roman name Paulus means "little." This is no mere word game, however. Paul really feels this way about himself, probably because he once persecuted the church (1 Cor. 15:9; Gal. 1:13). It is important to note, however, that while Paul may downplay himself, he never demeans the authority of his office as an apostle. In 4:1, for example, Paul uses the apostolic "I." He is not afraid to speak with direct authority. *riches.* Paul has named these riches in chapters 1 and 2. These include: redemption (1:7); forgiveness of sins (1:7); knowledge of his will (1:9–10); an inheritance (1:14,18); power (1:19); resurrection with Christ (2:5–6); enthronement with Christ (2:6); grace (2:7); kindness (2:7); citizenship in God's kingdom (2:19); and membership in God's family (2:19).

3:9 *to shed light.* In Greek, this verb means, "to enlighten." By it, Paul focuses on the condition of the lost (they are in darkness). Paul's original commission, given by Jesus on the Damascus Road, carried this idea: "I now send you to open their eyes that they may turn from darkness to light" (Acts 26:17–18). *for all.* Paul's ministry involves not just the evangelism of the Gentiles, but also the enlightenment of all people to God's marvelous plan.

3:10 *multi-faceted.* Literally, "multicolored." It was used to describe the riot of color found in a Greek flower garden. This is a fitting image of the depth and complexity of God and his plan for the church. It is reflected in the plan that he has for the multicolored, multinational, multiethnic church, newly forged in Jesus Christ. *made known ... to the rulers and authorities in the heavens.* At this point, Paul's vision soars to new heights as he declares the mystery of God and that the very supernatural powers themselves see what God is up to in the universe. They watch in fascination as traditional enemies (Jews and Gentiles) are drawn together into the church, and by this they learn about "the multifaceted wisdom of God."

3:12 *we have boldness, access, and confidence.* Another facet of this new reality is the fact that all people may now directly approach God. No longer is it necessary to come to God through a priest or other mediator. The sixteenth-century Reformers called this doctrine the "priesthood of all believers."

Paul's Prayer

Scripture Ephesians 3:14–21

LAST WEEK *Last week we were inspired by Paul's enthusiasm for the Gospel, and his total commitment to share it with others—even the Gentiles, the traditional enemies of the Jews. We were reminded that only by God's grace are we able to share the "mystery of the Messiah" with others. This week we will consider how prayer is a very powerful force, and that love for all God's people is not an option.*

 Ice-Breaker Connect With Your Group (15 minutes)

Prayer is an integral and beautiful part of the Christian's life. Many of us learned at least the basic principles of prayer as children, while others are just discovering prayer. Take turns sharing your unique experiences with prayer.

Leader
Open with a word of prayer, and then introduce any new people or visitors. Select one, two or all three of the Ice-Breaker questions to begin the study. Remember to stick closely to the three-part agenda and the time allowed for each segment.

1. Where is your favorite place to pray?

   ○ At church.
   ○ In bed.
   ○ Watching a sunset.
   ○ With a friend.
   ○ In my favorite chair.
   ○ While taking a walk.
   ○ Other _____.

2. When you were a child was there someone who prayed for you?

3. What prayer of yours has been answered?

Bible Study Read Scripture and Discuss (30 minutes)

Leader
Ask two group members, selected ahead of time, to read aloud the Scripture passage. Then discuss the Questions for Interaction, dividing into subgroups of three to six.

Paul once again falls to his knees in prayer for his readers, this time entreating the Lord to grant them the power of the Holy Spirit to become "rooted and firmly established in love" (v. 17). This is also a continuation of his central theme of unity, the unity that comes from being part of the body of Christ. Read Ephesians 3:14–21 and note how Paul describes the Messiah's love.

Paul's Prayer

Reader One: [14]For this reason I bow my knees before the Father [15]from whom every family in heaven and on earth is named. [16]I pray that He may grant you, according to the riches of His glory, to be strengthened with power through His Spirit in the inner man, [17]and that the Messiah may dwell in your hearts through faith. I pray that you, being rooted and firmly established in love, [18]may be able to comprehend with all the saints what is the breadth and width, height and depth, [19]and to know the Messiah's love that surpasses knowledge, so you may be filled with all the fullness of God.

Reader Two: [20]Now to Him who is able to do above and beyond all that we ask or think—according to the power that works in you— [21]to Him be glory in the church and in Christ Jesus to all generations, forever and ever. Amen.

Ephesians 3:14–21

Questions for Interaction

Leader
Refer to the Summary and Study Notes at the end of this session as needed. If 30 minutes is not enough time to answer all of the questions in this section, conclude the Bible Study by answering question 7.

1. When do you pray on a regular basis?

   ○ At bedtime.
   ○ Before meals.
   ○ Early in the morning.
   ○ While driving.
   ○ Before a test.
   ○ Other _____.

2. What do you usually pray for? How does that compare to what Paul prays for in today's passage?

3. What does it mean to have God's Holy Spirit "in the inner man" (v. 16)?

4. How does one become "firmly established in love" (v. 17)? Why does Paul feel that this is important?

5. What is the significance of Paul's reference to experiencing the love of Christ together "with all the saints" (see note on v. 18)? How could your church and small group do this more successfully?

6. How does a Christian become "filled with all the fullness of God" (v. 19)? What could help you to have a fuller faith?

7. If God is "able to do above and beyond all that we ask or think," (v. 20) how should that affect your prayer life? In what circumstances do you need to believe this right now?

Going Deeper   If your group has time and/or wants a challenge, go on to this question.

8. Paul prays in verses 18 and 19 that his readers "may be able to comprehend" the love of God which "surpasses knowledge." How can this be possible?

Caring Time Apply the Lesson and Pray for One Another (15 minutes)

When we pray, we should be bold in approaching the throne of God's grace because Jesus himself intercedes on our behalf. We should also remember to support one another in the same way, imitating Jesus and Paul by not praying only for our own needs. Take some time together now to pray for one another.

Leader
Be sure to save at least 15 minutes for this important time. Continue to encourage group members to invite new people to the group. Conclude the prayer time by praying for the Holy Spirit's leading in sharing the love of God with others.

1. What grade (A–F) would you give your prayer life today?

   ○ A—I feel really connect to God and spend time with him often.
   ○ B—I'm having devotions and think that he is hearing me.
   ○ C—I'm doing all right. I could be more regular.
   ○ D—I sometimes pray at meals.
   ○ F—I'm not sure God would recognize my voice.
   How would you like to improve that grade?

2. How do the members of this group show forth the love of God to you? How can we effectively show it to others outside this group?

3. Share the names of people you know who need the love of God in their lives, and then pray for those people as a group.

Notes on Ephesians 3:14–21

Summary: In this section, Paul completes the prayer he began in 3:1. There are three parts to the passage. In verses 14–15, Paul describes his manner of prayer and identifies the recipient of his petitions. In verses 16–19, Paul prays the prayer itself. In verses 20–21, Paul acknowledges the limitations of his prayer. In the prayer itself Paul asks for two main things—strength and knowledge—through three petitions.

3:14 *For this reason.* Paul repeats this phrase, first used in 3:1, and so picks up again the prayer he began back there. What motivates this prayer and shapes its content is what he said in chapters 1 and 2. There he pointed out God's intention to create a new body (the church) out of old enemies (Jew and Gentile). To be part of such a company is humanly impossible—unless a person is changed from within. So this is what Paul will pray for. He will pray that God the Holy Spirit will work in their inner being (v. 16); that God the Son will dwell in their hearts (v. 17); and that God the Father will fill them with his fullness (v. 19). *I bow my knees.* Jews typically stood when they prayed, as is seen in the Parable of the Pharisee and the Tax Collector (Luke 18:9–14; see also Matt. 6:5 and Mark 11:25). However, in times of great distress or deep feeling, one might kneel or lie prostrate. Ezra did this when he heard about the intermarriage between the people of Israel and the surrounding tribes (Ezra 9:3–5). In Gethsemane Jesus "fell with his face to the ground and prayed" (Matt. 26:39). *Father.* Paul seems to intend this title to have cosmic significance. God is the Father over all, whether they yet know him or not. In 4:6 he will call him "Father of all, who is above all and through all

and in all." Thus, as in 1:4–23 where Paul describes Christ in cosmic terms, so here he describes the Father in the same way.

3:15 *in heaven and on earth.* There are two parts to God's family: those on earth ("the church militant") and those in heaven ("the church triumphant"). *named.* In the early centuries, the act of naming was far more significant than merely giving a child a label to distinguish him or her from other children. To be named was, rather, to be given an identity and purpose. To be called by God's name is to be put under God's power and protection.

3:16 *strengthened with power.* Paul asks that Christians be fortified or invigorated within by the Holy Spirit. He asks that they experience this awesome power of God about which he has written so eloquently. Having been empowered, they are able to grasp the amazing love God has for them (v. 19). In other words, inner power makes inner knowledge possible. *inner man.* By this term, Paul may be referring to the deepest part of the human personality, where a person's true essence lies. The Greeks thought that there were three parts to one's inner being: reason—by which a person discerns right; conscience—

as a result of which a person strives for purity and holiness; and will—from which that person derives the ability to do what they know to be right. Furthermore, it would appear that it is through one's inner being that God is experienced. The Holy Spirit moves in power there. Christ dwells there. God the Father works there (vv. 19–20).

3:17 *dwell.* The Greek word used here, *katoikeo*, means "to settle down," or "to dwell" and it implies a permanent residency versus a temporary stopover. In other words, Christ has come to stay. In Colossians 1:27, Paul states that part of this mystery, which has been now revealed, is that Christ dwells within us. *faith.* This is the means by which a person is open to the indwelling Christ. *rooted and firmly established.* By his choice of these words, Paul hints at two metaphors through which the character of love is revealed. The Christian is to be anchored firmly in the soil of love just like a tree. The Christian is also to be set solidly on the foundation of love just like a well-constructed house. (The second word in Greek is literally "grounded.") *love.* *Agape* love is selfless giving to others, regardless of how one feels. Such love is the foundation upon which the church will grow. Otherwise, the newly redeemed enemies would remain enemies.

3:18 *with all the saints.* Knowing the love of Christ is vital for the whole church. Christ's love cannot, by definition, be known in isolation. Love, to be love, must be experienced and expressed. Love is the fuel by which the church is sustained and grows. *breadth and width, height and depth.* Paul expresses the magnitude of God's love.

3:19 *to know the Messiah's love that surpasses knowledge.* Paul uses extravagant language to make his point. He prays that they will know what can't be known! God's love is such that limited human faculties can never grasp its fullness (though Christians must strive to do so). *the fullness of God.* It is possible to translate this phrase two ways. If the possessive (genitive) is objective, then God's fullness refers to the gifts of grace that he gives to people. If it is subjective, then God's fullness refers to that which fills God himself. In fact, it is probably this latter meaning that is intended. Christians are to be filled with the very perfection of God himself.

3:20 Paul prays because God is able to do what is asked. In fact, he is able to do much more than we can either ask or even imagine, because of his great power. *above and beyond.* By this Paul intends to convey that given our limited knowledge, we cannot even pray for all that God can (and will) do for us. *the power that works in you.* This power is within individual Christians and within the body as a whole. This is the power Paul has been describing.

Unity in the Body

Scripture Ephesians 4:1–16

LAST WEEK *In our previous session, we focused on the incomprehensible power of prayer, and were urged to share the love of God with all the saints. We were reminded to pray for the Holy Spirit to give us strength and understanding. This week we will discover that every single one of the saints is a vitally important part of God's body.*

 Ice-Breaker Connect With Your Group (15 minutes)

Growing up can be a painful experience, but those experiences help us to mature and become successful adults. Take turns sharing your experiences with growing and maturing.

1. What did you do in high school that taught you teamwork?

   ○ Team sports.
   ○ Science projects.
   ○ Yearbook Staff.
   ○ Local gang.
   ○ Marching band.
   ○ Other _____.

2. What was one significant moment in your life when you realized that you were grown up?

3. Whom do you admire as being spiritually mature?

Leader
Open with a word of prayer, and then introduce any new people or visitors. Select from the Ice-Breaker questions to begin the study. If there are new members, then discuss all three to help them get acquainted.

Bible Study Read Scripture and Discuss (30 minutes)

Leader
Ask two group members, selected ahead of time, to read aloud the Scripture passage. Have one person read verses 1–8; and the other read verses 9–16. Then discuss the Questions for Interaction, dividing into subgroups of three to six.

In this section, we are called upon to "walk worthy of the calling" (v. 1) that we have received. Paul explains that this walk includes the high priority of maintaining unity within the body of Christ, each person recognizing his or her place in that body and learning to love others. Read Ephesians 4:1–16 and note the importance of the Holy Spirit in helping us to walk in love and peace.

Unity in the Body

Reader One: 4 I, therefore, the prisoner in the Lord, urge you to walk worthy of the calling you have received, ²with all humility and gentleness, with patience, accepting one another in love, ³diligently keeping the unity of the Spirit with the peace that binds us. ⁴There is one body and one Spirit, just as you were called to one hope at your calling; ⁵one Lord, one faith, one baptism, ⁶one God and Father of all, who is above all and through all and in all. ⁷Now grace was given to each one of us according to the measure of the Messiah's gift. ⁸For it says:

When He ascended on high, He took prisoners into captivity;

He gave gifts to people.

Reader Two: ⁹But what does "He ascended" mean except that He descended to the lower parts of the earth? ¹⁰The One who descended is the same as the One who ascended far above all the heavens, that He might fill all things. ¹¹And He personally gave some to be apostles, some prophets, some evangelists, some pastors and teachers, ¹²for the training of the saints in the work of ministry, to build up the body of Christ, ¹³until we all reach unity in the faith and in the knowledge of God's Son, growing into a mature man with a stature measured by Christ's fullness. ¹⁴Then we will no longer be little children, tossed by the waves and blown around by every wind of teaching, by human cunning with cleverness in the techniques of deceit. ¹⁵But speaking the truth in love, let us grow in every way into Him who is the head—Christ. ¹⁶From Him the whole body, fitted and knit together by every supporting ligament, promotes the growth of the body for building up itself in love by the proper working of each individual part.

Ephesians 4:1–16

Questions for Interaction

Leader
Refer to the Summary and Study Notes at the end of this session as needed. If 30 minutes is not enough time to answer all of the questions in this section, conclude the Bible Study by answering questions 6 and 7.

1. Of the four jobs in a church leadership team that Paul describes, which job are you best qualified for?

   ○ Apostle (pioneer and church planter).
   ○ Prophet (motivator and encourager).
   ○ Evangelist (soul winner).
   ○ Pastor/teacher (trainer and coach).
   How can you "walk worthy" of that calling (v. 1)?

2. What is God's purpose in giving gifts to his people? Why is it important that each part of "the body" does its work?

3. What does it mean to be "speaking the truth in love" in verse 15? How is this different from just speaking the truth? How is it different from not speaking the truth in order to be "loving"?

4. Why does Paul emphasize that Christ "descended" (vv. 9–10)? How does this set a standard for the love that his followers must show one another?

5. What is the picture of the church in verses 14–16 that Paul prays for? Why is it so vitally important that Christians stay connected to a church?

6. When have you tried to live apart from the church? What happened? What could you do now to become even more "fitted and knit together" (v. 16) with your church?

7. As an "individual part" of Christ's body, how well are you working?

   ○ Strong and supple.
   ○ A bit stiff today.
   ○ Getting a bit flabby.
   ○ I'm on bed rest.
   ○ I'm in the grave looking up.
   ○ Other _____.

8. What does Paul mean in verse 13 that we are to have a "stature measured by Christ's fullness"? How can believers make sure they become spiritually mature?

 Caring Time Apply the Lesson and Pray for One Another **(15 minutes)**

It is vital to the health of God's church that Christians work together as a unified group. Spend some time together now, sharing and praying in the unity of the Holy Spirit.

1. What was the high point of last week for you? What was the low point?

2. How are you doing at your own "body" exercises, such as personal study and prayer?

3. What have you appreciated about the functioning body of Christ in this group?

Leader
Continue to encourage group members to invite new people to the group. Remind everyone that this group is for learning and sharing, but also for reaching out to others. Conclude the group prayer by asking God to help each group member to grow and function as a healthy part of Christ's body.

NEXT WEEK *Today we considered how the body of Christ needs every single member to be functioning and healthy if the body is to be healthy. In the coming week, make a point to encourage someone else in your group by saying "thank you" for his or her part in the body. Next week we will be challenged as members of that body to become more and more like Christ.*

Summary: Paul begins the second half of his epistle by calling for all Christians to lead "a life worthy" of the grand plan of which they have been called to be a part. Thus he signals his shift in focus from doctrine (chapters 1–3) to duty (chapters 4–6); from exposition of the mystery of God to exhortation to live in a way that is consistent with what they know to be true. Paul begins chapter 4 by focusing on those attitudes, actions and insights that foster unity within the body (vv. 1–6). Then he shifts his emphasis to the diversity of gifts and functions within the one body (vv. 7–13). He ends by pointing to the maturity produced by such diversity within unity (vv. 14–16).

4:1 *the prisoner in the Lord.* In 3:1, Paul described himself as "the prisoner of Christ Jesus"—reflecting the fact that while legally he was the prisoner of Rome, spiritually he was the prisoner of Christ Jesus. Here in 4:1, he maintains the same dual insight—he is a prisoner, but his true (and willing) bondage is not to Caesar but to Christ. *I ... urge you.* The first half of the book was a long prayer for the church, and an exposition of how it was created. Paul, with the full weight of his apostolic authority ("I"), exhorts and beseeches all who are part of this church to live a new style of life. Having expounded upon what God did, he now explains what they must do. Stylistically, Paul moves from the indicative ("This is the way things are") to the imperative ("This is what must be done"). *walk worthy.* This is the theme of the remainder of Ephesians. Having described the creation by God of this new society, Paul now defines the lifestyle of this new race of people (Christians).

4:2 Paul identifies the five qualities of life that promote unity between people: humility, gentleness, patience, mutual forbearance and love. *Humility.* Humility is an absence of pride and self-assertion (both of which are sources of discord), based upon accurate self-knowledge and on an understanding of the God-given worth of others. Humility is the key to the growth of healthy relationships between people. *gentleness.* Paul is not urging people to be timid and without convictions. Gentleness is the quality of consideration and kindness. It implies firmness, but is full of sweetness and tenderness. *patience.* Patience is long suffering. *accepting one another.* This is the kind of tolerance of the faults of others that springs from humility, gentleness and patience.

4:3 *diligently keeping.* What Paul is saying is: "Work zealously at maintaining in visible form what has already been achieved for you by Christ and is therefore a fact." *unity.* This is the goal of the five virtues. It is the close bonding of people to one another. While verse 4 indicates that what is in view is the unity of the Christian church, these same attitudes build unity in all kinds of relationships: within marriage, across generations and between groups. *the peace that binds.* This peace has been made possible through Jesus Christ, who first reconciled humanity to God (bringing peace with God) and then reconciled people to one another (creating a bond of peace between them).

4:4–6 The unity that Paul is urging is based upon the threefold work of the triune God. God the Holy Spirit creates the one body (v. 3). God the Son brings hope, faith and baptism to this body (vv. 4b–5), while God the Father fills the body (v. 6).

4:4 *one body and one Spirit.* It is the indwelling Holy Spirit that maintains this single body—the church—within which Jew and Gentile come together.

4:5 *one Lord.* Since all Christians are indwelt by the same person and filled with the same power, there is a deep and natural affinity of one Christian for another. The title "Lord" means, "Master." The "Lord" is the one from whom direction is received and obeyed.

4:7 *grace.* In 2:1–10, Paul discussed saving grace. Here, his focus is on the grace by which these redeemed men and women serve Christ and his church (serving grace).

4:8 Paul quotes Psalm 68:18, which describes the triumphal procession of a conquering Jewish king up Mount Zion and into Jerusalem. The king is followed by a procession of prisoners in chains. As he marches up the hill, he is given gifts of tribute and in turn disperses gifts of booty. Paul uses this verse to describe Christ's ascension into heaven. The captives that follow along behind him are the principalities and powers that he has defeated (1:20–22; Col. 2:15). The gifts that the conquering Christ disperses are gifts of ministry given to his followers.

4:9 *descended.* Paul is referring to Christ's incarnation, whereby he came down from heaven and invaded space and time (Phil. 2:5–11). It has been suggested that this may be a reference to preaching the Gospel to the dead as mention by Peter (1 Peter 3:19; 4:6) or to the humiliation of the death on the cross.

4:11 This is one of several lists of gifts (Rom. 12:6–8; 1 Cor. 12:8–10,28–30). No single list is exhaustive, defining all the gifts; each is illustrative. The emphasis in this list is on the teaching gifts. *apostles.* Paul probably had in mind the small group of individuals who had seen the resurrected Christ, and had been commissioned by him to launch his church (Acts 1:21–22; 1 Cor. 9:1). *prophets.* In contrast to teachers who relied upon the Old Testament Scripture and the teaching of Jesus to instruct others, prophets offered words of instruction, exhortation and admonition, which were immediate and unpremeditated. Their source was direct revelation from God. *evangelists.* In the early centuries of the church, these were the men and women who moved from place to place, telling the Gospel story to those who had not heard it and/or believed it. While all Christians are called upon to be witnesses of the Gospel, the reference here is to those with the special gift of evangelism. This gift is the ability to make the Gospel clear and convincing to people. *pastors and teachers.* The way in which this is expressed in Greek indicates that these two functions reside in one person. In a day when books were rare and expensive, it was the task of the pastor/teacher not only to look after the welfare of the flock (the title "pastor" means, literally, "shepherd") but to preserve the Christian tradition and instruct people in it.

4:12 *training.* These teaching gifts are to be used to train everyone in the church so that each Christian is capable of ministry. In 3:12, Paul taught the concept of the "priesthood of all believers." Here, he teaches "the ministry of all believers."

4:13–16 The aim of all these gifts is to produce maturity. Maturity is, in turn, vital to unity—the theme with which Paul began this section.

4:15 *speaking the truth in love.* Christians are to stand for both truth and love. Both are necessary. Truth without love becomes harsh. Love without truth becomes weak.

Children of Light

Scripture Ephesians 4:17–32

LAST WEEK *In last week's session, we considered how important each person is to the body of Christ. We were reminded to take our calling seriously and keep our spiritual life healthy. Today we will be challenged to live more like Christ, rooting out "all wickedness" from our lives and being careful not to grieve the Holy Spirit.*

Ice-Breaker Connect With Your Group (15 minutes)

Learning to change is not always as easy as putting on new clothes. Often it is very difficult to change, as we've all experienced with New Year's resolutions that didn't last for long. Take turns sharing your experiences with trying to change your behavior.

Leader
Open with a word of prayer, and then introduce any new people or visitors. Select one, two or all three of the Ice-Breaker questions to begin the study.

1. When it comes to clothes, which of the following best describes you?

    ○ Bold and daring.
    ○ Quiet and reserved.
    ○ Bright and refreshing.
    ○ Elegant and refined.
    ○ New and fashionable.
    ○ Old and comfortable.
    How has your style of clothes changed since you were in high school or college?

2. What was your most recent New Year's resolution? What happened? If you don't make New Year's resolutions, why not?

3. When it comes to getting angry, is your fuse short or long? How would you like to change?

Bible Study Read Scripture and Discuss (30 minutes)

Leader
Select three group members ahead of time to read aloud the Scripture passage. Then discuss the Questions for Interaction, dividing into subgroups of three to six.

Paul continues his exhortations to the Ephesian church to learn to live as Jesus lived, putting away the things of darkness that they once pursued and learning to pursue instead the things of light. Read Ephesians 4:17–32 and note how the Christian lifestyle should be distinctly different from the rest of the world.

Children of Light

Reader One: [17]Therefore, I say this and testify in the Lord: You should no longer walk as the Gentiles walk, in the futility of their thoughts. [18]They are darkened in their understanding, excluded from the life of God, because of the ignorance that is in them and because of the hardness of their hearts. [19]They became callous and gave themselves over to promiscuity for the practice of every kind of impurity with a desire for more and more.

Reader Two: [20]But that is not how you learned about the Messiah, [21]assuming you heard Him and were taught by Him, because the truth is in Jesus: [22]you took off your former way of life, the old man that is corrupted by deceitful desires; [23]you are being renewed in the spirit of your minds; [24]you put on the new man, the one created according to God's likeness in righteousness and purity of the truth.

Reader Three: [25]Since you put away lying, Speak the truth, each one to his neighbor, because we are members of one another. [26]Be angry and do not sin. Don't let the sun go down on your anger, [27]and don't give the Devil an opportunity. [28]The thief must no longer steal. Instead, he must do honest work with his own hands, so that he has something to share with anyone in need. [29]No rotten talk should come from your mouth, but only what is good for the building up of someone in need, in order to give grace to those who hear. [30]And don't grieve God's Holy Spirit, who sealed you for the day of redemption. [31]All bitterness, anger and wrath, insult and slander must be removed from you, along with all wickedness. [32]And be kind and compassionate to one another, forgiving one another, just as God also forgave you in Christ.

Ephesians 4:17–32

Questions for Interaction

Leader
Refer to the Summary and Study Notes at the end of this session as needed. If 30 minutes is not enough time to answer all of the questions in this section, conclude the Bible Study by answering questions 6 and 7.

1. Growing up, what is a behavior that your parents insisted you do?

   ○ Being quiet in church.
   ○ Getting to bed at a certain time.
   ○ Brushing my teeth every day.
   ○ Doing my chores.
   ○ Being polite to relatives.
   ○ Other _____.

   How well did you do at obeying your parents?

2. Why can't the "Gentiles" (unbelievers) change their behavior and live a life that is pleasing to God (vv. 17–19)?

3. What does Paul mean by taking off "the old man" (v. 22) and putting on "the new man" (v. 24)?

4. How are we "renewed in the spirit of" our minds (v. 23)? Why is this so important in being able to "put on the new man"?

5. What exactly is "rotten talk"? What sort of talk "is good for the building up of someone in need"? What grade (A–F) would you give yourself on putting verse 29 into practice this last week?

6. How have your attitudes, actions and thoughts changed since turning your life over to God?

7. Which of the commands for Christian living given in this passage seems to be the most challenging to you right now?

Going Deeper If your group has time and/or wants a challenge, go on to this question.

8. How exactly is a person to accomplish verse 31, removing "all bitterness, anger and wrath, insult and slander ... along with all wickedness"? How can we as a group work on this together?

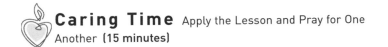

Caring Time
Apply the Lesson and Pray for One Another (15 minutes)

Leader
Have you been encouraging your group about their mission—perhaps by sharing the dream of multiplying into two groups at the end of this study of Ephesians?

One of the deeds of "darkness" that we all struggle with is anger and resentment. Through sharing and prayer help one another to remain unified in the love of Christ.

1. Are you struggling with anger toward anyone at the moment? How can you not "let the sun go down on your anger" (v. 26)?

2. Is there someone that you need to ask for forgiveness? How can the group help you accomplish this?

3. What praise items can you share to help build up the group?

NEXT WEEK *Today we were challenged to become more and more like Christ, purging from our lives "all wickedness." In the coming week, focus on rooting out one area of weakness in your life, whether it be rotten talk, bitterness or any other issue raised here, especially the one you mentioned when answering question 7. Next week we will be challenged once again to live a Christian lifestyle, as we strive to become imitators of God.*

Notes on Ephesians 4:17–32

Summary: Paul continues his exposition of the "walk worthy of the calling" (4:1). Having urged the Christians to cultivate unity, he now urges them to cultivate purity. In shifting his topic, Paul also shifts his focus. In discussing unity, his focus was on the Christian community. In discussing purity, his focus will be on the Christian individual.

4:17 *in the Lord.* He is writing to them not on his own authority, but in the Lord's name. This is Paul the apostle speaking, not Paul the man. *as the Gentiles walk.* Paul begins this section on purity of life by describing the typical Gentile lifestyle from which Christians must flee. The Gentile lifestyle is described in a fashion parallel to Paul's more extended exposition in Romans 1:18–32. In both sections, the pagan spiral into darkness begins with hardness of

heart that leads to distorted thinking, which in turn brings alienation from God, out of which flows a consuming sensuality. *the futility of their thoughts.* Paul emphasizes the connection between thought and behavior. Right thinking does matter if a person is to get on with right living.

4:18 *hardness of their hearts.* The center of their being (the heart) has become "stone-like" or "petrified." The word Paul uses is *poros* and it means "marble."

4:19 *promiscuity ... impurity ... desire.* By these three nouns, Paul describes what pagan life has evolved into. Such forms of overindulgence stand in contrast to the purity and holiness which ought to characterize the Christian life.

4:20–21 *learned about the Messiah ... you heard Him ... taught by Him.* Paul uses three phrases to describe how the Christian comes to learn the right way of thinking. The first phrase, "learned about the Messiah," focuses on the fact that Christ is the subject matter of their education. The second phrase, "you heard Him," emphasizes that Jesus himself is the teacher. The third phrase, "taught by Him," makes the point that Jesus is the very environment within which their learning takes place. The path to right thinking (and hence, to right living) is through the school of the Messiah.

4:22–24 *took off ... put on.* Paul develops a clothing metaphor here. At conversion, the Christian sheds the old, ragged, filthy garment and puts on a fresh, new cloak.

old man ... new man. In conversion, the Christian puts the old, sinful nature and puts on the very life of Christ himself.

4:23 *renewed.* The verbs translated "took off" and "put on" are in the aorist tense, that is, they signify a completed past action. This exchange of natures occurs at conversion. However, here the verb tense is a present infinitive, "be made new" or "be renewed," indicating the need for ongoing, continual renewal. *the spirit of your minds.* Again, the emphasis is on right thinking in order to be able to live right.

4:25–32 Paul now gives a few concrete examples of what this new lifestyle looks like. It is charac-

terized by truth (v. 25), by proper control of anger (vv. 26–27), by honest labor (v. 28), by edifying talk (vv. 29–30), and by love (vv. 31–32).

4:25 *Since.* Having just described what is indeed so for Christians (they have a new self which bears the marks of God's very nature—righteousness and holiness), Paul will now describe specifically what their lifestyle ought to be. This verse is a model for how Paul discusses each of the six topics. He begins with the negative deed, in this case, falsehood. (In Greek, the word is literally "the lie.") Then he sets in contrast the positive virtue that he commends, in this case, truthful speech. Then he gives a reason for this command. Here, it is that we are all neighbors. In fact, we are even closer than that: "we are members of one another." Lies destroy fellowship. Unity must be built on trust, and trust comes through truth.

4:26 *Be angry.* Paul recognizes that there is such a thing as legitimate anger. Paul says in 5:6 that God experiences anger, though the translation obscures this meaning. (Although the phrase in 5:6b is rendered as "God's wrath," the same word is used there which is here translated "anger.") Jesus was angry (Mark 3:5). There are certain situations in which anger is the only honest response. For Christians to deny their anger is dangerous and self-defeating. But once admitted, anger is to be dealt with, and so Paul identifies four ways to deal with anger. First, "Be angry and do not sin." What is the source of the anger? Is it wounded pride or real wrong? Is it spite or is it injustice? In verse 31, Paul will point out that unrighteous anger is to be gotten rid of. Second, "Don't let the sun go down on your anger." We are to deal with it quickly. Do not nurse anger and let it grow. Third, do not let anger develop into resentment. Be reconciled if possible. Fourth, do not let Satan exploit your anger, turning it into hostility (or using it to disrupt fellowship).

4:28 It is not enough simply to stop stealing; the thief must also start working.

4:29–30 From the use of one's hands, Paul turns to the use of one's mouth. The word translated "rotten" is used to describe spoiled fruit (Matt. 12:33). Instead of rancid words that wound others, the words of Christians ought to edify ("building up"), be appropriate ("of someone in need"), bring grace and not grieve the Holy Spirit (by unholy words).

4:31 Paul identifies six negative attitudes which must be erased from the Christian life. *bitter-ness.* Spiteful, long-standing resentment. *anger and wrath.* These two attitudes are related. The first is a more immediate flare-up, while the latter is a more long-term, sullen hostility. This is not the "righteous anger" Paul dealt with in verse 26. *insult and slander.* Saying untrue and hurtful things about a person.

4:32 In contrast to the negative attitudes listed in verse 31, here Paul identifies a set of positive attitudes that ought to characterize the Christian. Instead of bitterness, anger, wrath, insult, slander and wickedness the Christian is to display kindness, compassion and forgiveness.

Imitators of God

Scripture Ephesians 5:1–21

LAST WEEK *In last week's session, Paul reminded us once again to live more like Christ, rooting out all wickedness. Instead of bitterness, anger, wrath, insult and slander the Christian is to display kindness, compassion and forgiveness. Today Paul continues on the theme of deliberately choosing to imitate the Father.*

 Ice-Breaker Connect With Your Group (15 minutes)

Imitation is the highest form of flattery, and we all do it. Some of us like to imitate rock stars, some of us are content just to try and carry a tune. Paul tells us today to be "imitators of God." Take turns sharing some of your experiences about imitating others.

Leader
Open with a word of prayer, and then introduce any new people. Select one, two or all three of the Ice-Breaker questions to begin the study.

1. Who did you most want to be like in high school?

    ○ The most popular kid in school.
    ○ A celebrity.
    ○ My favorite teacher.
    ○ An athlete.
    ○ My youth group leader.
    ○ Other _____.

2. What famous person can you imitate? Demonstrate for the group.

3. What famous person, contemporary or historical, would you most like to be like today (other than Jesus)?

Bible Study Read Scripture and Discuss (30 minutes)

Leader
Select three group members ahead of time to read aloud the Scripture passage. Have one member read verses 1–5; another read verses 6–14; and the third person read verses 15–21. Then discuss the Questions for Interaction, dividing into subgroups of three to six.

Continuing the theme of walking in the light, Paul now exhorts his readers to learn godliness by the simple expedient of imitating God. He becomes quite explicit as to what this entails, as the followers of Jesus need to turn their backs on the things of the world. Read Ephesians 5:1–21 and note the four incentives Paul lists for Christian living.

Imitators of God

Reader One: 5 Therefore, be imitators of God, as dearly loved children. ²And walk in love, as the Messiah also loved us and gave Himself for us, a sacrificial and fragrant offering to God. ³But sexual immorality and any impurity or greed should not even be heard of among you, as is proper for saints. ⁴And coarse and foolish talking or crude joking are not suitable, but rather giving thanks. ⁵For know and recognize this: no sexually immoral or impure or greedy person, who is an idolater, has an inheritance in the kingdom of the Messiah and of God.

Reader Two: ⁶Let no one deceive you with empty arguments, for because of these things God's wrath is coming on the disobedient. ⁷Therefore, do not become their partners. ⁸For you were once darkness, but now you are light in the Lord. Walk as children of light— ⁹for the fruit of the light results in all goodness, righteousness, and truth— ¹⁰discerning what is pleasing to the Lord. ¹¹Don't participate in the fruitless works of darkness, but instead, expose them. ¹²For it is shameful even to mention what is done by them in secret. ¹³Everything exposed by the light is made clear, ¹⁴for what makes everything clear is light. Therefore it is said:
> Get up, sleeper, and rise up from the dead,
> and the Messiah will shine on you.

Reader Three: ¹⁵Pay careful attention, then, to how you walk—not as unwise people but as wise— ¹⁶making the most of the time, because the days are evil. ¹⁷So don't be foolish, but understand what the Lord's will is. ¹⁸And don't get drunk with wine, which leads to reckless actions, but be filled with the Spirit:
> ¹⁹speaking to one another in psalms, hymns, and spiritual songs,
>   singing and making music to the Lord in your heart,
> ²⁰giving thanks always for everything
>   to God the Father in the name of our Lord Jesus Christ,
> ²¹submitting to one another in the fear of Christ.

Ephesians 5:1–21

Questions for Interaction

Leader
Refer to the Summary and Study Notes at the end of this session as needed. If 30 minutes is not enough time to answer all of the questions in this section, conclude the Bible Study by answering question 7.

1. What rules did your parents have regarding "forbidden language"? What happened if you spoke the unspeakable?

   ○ Washed my mouth out with soap.
   ○ Got the evil eye.
   ○ Grounded.
   ○ Time out.
   ○ The cold shoulder.
   ○ No big thing.
   ○ Nobody would have noticed.
   ○ Other _____.

2. What constitutes "coarse and foolish talking" and "crude joking" (v. 4)? What are we to talk about instead?

3. This is the second time that Paul has honed in on controlling the tongue. Why do you think he makes such an issue of it?

4. Why does Paul state that greedy people are idolaters (v. 5)?

5. According to verses 8–14, what should be a Christian's attitude and response to X-rated TV, pornography on the Internet and "adult" literature? How far should a Christian go in exposing the darkness?

6. What characterizes someone who is filled with the Spirit (vv. 18–21)?

7. As you look back over your life since giving your life to God, where have you seen the greatest change?

   ○ In my motives.
   ○ In my desires.
   ○ In my language.
   ○ In my values.
   ○ In the way I treat others.
   ○ Other _____.

Going Deeper   If your group has time and/or wants a challenge, go on to this question.

8. Note that in verse 8 Paul does not say "you were once in darkness," but rather "you were once darkness, but now you are light." What does this mean?

Caring Time Apply the Lesson and Pray for One
Another (15 minutes)

For us to be able to "be imitators of God," we need more than study—we need support and encouragement. This is your time to give that to each other. Share your responses to the following questions before closing in prayer.

Leader
Have you identified someone in the group that could be a leader for a new small group when your group divides? How could you encourage and mentor that person?

1. Are there any areas of coarse speech or impurity that the Lord would have you change?

2. Would you view your own life as being "filled with the Spirit" (v. 18)? What areas of your life do you need to ask the Holy Spirit to control?

3. Is there someone in this group whose life does exemplify the presence of the Holy Spirit? If so, let them know.

NEXT WEEK *Today we were challenged by Paul to rid our lives of all impurity, greed and sexual immorality. To accomplish this he calls us to control our speech and to be filled by the Holy Spirit. In the coming week, ask God each day to help you imitate him more and more in each of these areas, especially the ones you mentioned in question 2 in the Caring Time. Next week we will be challenged by some teachings on marriage that defy what our modern culture would have us believe.*

Summary: Paul continues his commentary on what the Christian lifestyle ought to look like in contrast to the pagan lifestyle that so many of them lived out prior to coming to faith. He begins by urging the imitation of God by living a life of love in contrast to the life of lust they once knew. Then he moves to the whole question of incentives. Why should a person live a life in imitation of God? In verses 5–21, Paul identifies four incentives for Christian living.

5:1–2 If the Ephesians want to know what the Christian lifestyle is all about, they simply have to look at how God lives. They can see this by looking at Jesus, who is God-come-in-the-flesh. In Jesus, they will see that the divine way is the way of self-giving love. This is the basic model for the Christian life. If one lives in love, then all the specific behaviors Paul has been pointing out will flow naturally.

5:3–4 From love, Paul turns to lust. In these verses, in contrast to the Christian way that he just described, he defines the pagan way that they might be tempted to follow. Christians must not give in to sexual immorality (even though such behavior was rampant among Gentiles in the first century).

5:3 *sexual immorality/impurity.* These two words cover all forms of promiscuous sexual behavior among married or unmarried people. *not even be heard of.* Even naming such sins (in word or thought) is harmful.

5:4 *crude joking.* Vulgar talk is out of place, because it demeans God's good gift of sex (which is a subject for thanksgiving, not joking).

5:5–21 Paul's subject in verse 5 is still overindulgence, but he has moved into a new phase of his argument. Having just identified six specific sets of behavior that ought to characterize Christians, now he will point out four incentives to proper living. Paul has moved from model to motive. The four incentives are the fact of judgment (vv. 5–7), the implications of being a child of light (vv. 8–14), the nature of wisdom (vv. 15–17), and the filling of the Holy Spirit (vv. 18–21).

5:5 *greedy person.* The reference is to the sexually greedy person. *idolater.* When vice has become an obsession, it functions in a person's life as a "god" (or idol), drawing forth passionate commitment of time and energy.

5:6 *empty arguments.* Influenced by Greek philosophy that minimized the importance of the body in contrast to the spirit, some wrongly taught that the sins of the body did not matter. *God's wrath is coming.* Those who live a committed and public life of self-indulgent sensuality without repenting will be called to account.

5:8 *darkness/light.* Darkness represents what is secret and evil, and is out of touch with God's purposes. Light stands for goodness and truth, and for obedience to God, which issues in openness and transparency.

5:9 *fruit of the light.* Paul defines these as "goodness" (the generosity of spirit that comes of doing God's will), "righteousness" (just actions toward others), and "truth" (honest dealings with others).

5:11 In contrast to "the fruit of the light" are "fruitless works of darkness." The Christian's response to "deeds of darkness" is, on the negative side, to "have nothing to do" with them.

On the positive side, the Christian is to "expose" these deeds. The effect of light will be to reveal the ugliness of sin.

5:15–17 A third impulse to Christian living is wisdom. Paul assumes that wisdom will teach one how to live (i.e., wisdom is practical and not merely theoretical); and that it is better to be wise than a fool.

5:18 *drunk.* Be filled with the Spirit not with "spirits." *be filled.* This is a command, not an option. It is issued to all Christians (in Greek, it is plural). The present tense of the verb signifies continuous action ("go on being filled"), and

since the command is in the passive voice, it means, "let the Spirit fill you."

5:19 Public worship is in view here and the aim is mutual edification.

5:20 *giving thanks ... for everything.* This is acknowledging God's unchanging goodness and complete control. Even in circumstances which we cannot understand or see any good in can be used by God for good.

5:21 *submitting to one another.* Another aspect of being filled with the Spirit involves mutual submission within the Christian community.

Wives and Husbands

Scripture Ephesians 5:22–33

> **LAST WEEK** *"Therefore, be imitators of God" (5:1). Last week Paul reminded us that we must deliberately seek to imitate God in all areas of our lives. We are to bring light into a darkened world through our speech, our sexual conduct and all aspects of our Spirit-filled lives. Today we will be challenged with some teachings on marriage that go directly against much of what our culture would have us believe.*

 Ice-Breaker Connect With Your Group (15 minutes)

Leader
Open with a word of prayer, and then introduce any new people. Select one, two or all three Ice-Breaker questions to begin the study.

Marriage and family are the backbone of any stable society. But for most of us, building a good marriage and happy home can be a mysterious undertaking. Take turns sharing some of your own thoughts and experiences about love and marriage.

1. What is your favorite love story (real or fictional)?

   ○ Love Story.
   ○ Gone With the Wind.
   ○ Sound of Music.
   ○ My parents' story.
   ○ Other _____.

2. What married couple best illustrates to you what a good marriage can be?

3. If married, when is your anniversary? What number is coming up next?

Bible Study Read Scripture and Discuss (30 minutes)

Paul now turns his attention to very personal matters, addressing the sort of home life that should be exhibited by followers of Christ. Husbands are to love their wives as Christ loved the church; wives are to submit to their husbands as to the Lord. Paul grounds these teachings in another mystery, the mystery of Christ and his church. Here again, these exhortations are essential to the unity of Christ's body, the church. Read Ephesians 5:22–33 and note how special the marriage relationship is in the eyes of God.

Leader
Select two members of the group ahead of time to read aloud the Scripture passage. Then discuss the Questions for Interaction, dividing into subgroups of three to six.

Wives and Husbands

Reader One: [22]Wives, submit to your own husbands as to the Lord, [23]for the husband is head of the wife as also Christ is head of the church. He is the Savior of the body. [24]Now as the church submits to Christ, so wives should submit to their husbands in everything.

Reader Two: [25]Husbands, love your wives, just as also Christ loved the church and gave Himself for her, [26]to make her holy, cleansing her in the washing of water by the word. [27]He did this to present the church to Himself in splendor, without spot or wrinkle or any such thing, but holy and blameless. [28]In the same way, husbands should love their wives as their own bodies. He who loves his wife loves himself. [29]For no one ever hates his own flesh, but provides and cares for it, just as Christ does for the church, [30]since we are members of His body.

Reader One: [31] For this reason a man will leave his father and mother
and be joined to his wife,
and the two will become one flesh.

Reader Two: [32]This mystery is profound, but I am talking about Christ and the church. [33]To sum up, each one of you is to love his wife as himself, and the wife is to respect her husband.

Ephesians 5:22–33

Questions for Interaction

Leader
Refer to the Summary and Study Notes at the end of this session as needed. If 30 minutes is not enough time to answer all of the questions in this section, conclude the Bible Study by answering question 7.

1. In your own opinion, what are the two most important ingredients needed to make a good marriage?

   O Commitment.
   O Common interests.
   O Friendship.
   O Respect.
   O Love.
   O Spiritual unity.
   O Other _____.

2. What things does Paul suggest are necessary to make a good marriage?

3. Paul's injunction that wives must submit to their husbands is very countercultural today. What does it mean for a wife to submit to her husband?

4. Paul's injunction that husbands must love their wives as much as they love their own bodies is also countercultural. What does this command mean for husbands? If a husband loves his wife to that degree, what effect will it have on his wife?

5. The model for marriage is Christ himself. As he went to the cross in obedience to the Father, and out of love for us, how does this help us to understand a husband's role? A wife's role?

6. In your own words, how would you explain the main goal of a Christian marriage?

7. What can you take from this passage that will help you be a better spouse (or potential spouse)?

Going Deeper   If your group has time and/or wants a challenge, go on to this question.

8. Note the verbs Paul uses in this passage: husbands must "love," wives must "submit" and "respect." Why are these difficult for couples to do? Why does Paul not reverse them?

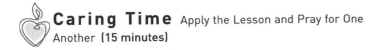

Caring Time Apply the Lesson and Pray for One Another (15 minutes)

Leader
Conclude the prayer time today by asking God for guidance in determining the future mission and outreach of this group.

Good marriages require a great deal of work, and it is important that the church (and Bible study groups) work to support and protect the marriages of their members. Take some time together now to pray for and support one another in this vital area.

1. If you are married, what is one thing about your spouse that makes you proud or for which you are very thankful?

2. What is one thing that you feel you should change to please your spouse?

3. How can the group pray for you regarding the area of submission to Christ in your life?

NEXT WEEK *Today we examined some difficult teachings about marriage, teachings that go against much of what our modern culture would have us believe. In the coming week, prayerfully strive to put these into practice in order to please the Father: wives, submit to your husbands; husbands, love your wives as Christ loves the church. Those who are not married should strive to submit to Christ in every area of their life. Next week we will learn how to be godly whether we are in authority or under authority.*

Summary: Paul turns to the need for quality relationships at home and at work. He focuses aspects of a crucial relationship: that between husband and wife. After addressing the role of wives in three verses, Paul devotes nine verses to explain to men the kind of self-giving love that is required of them.

5:22 The verb in 5:21 ("submit") is linked grammatically both backward to 5:18 and forward to this verse. Looking backward, "submit" is the last of four present participles that describe what is involved in being filled with the Spirit. Looking forward, "submit" provides the verb for this verse, which has no verb of its own.

5:23 *as.* The reason why wives should submit to husbands is given by means of a simile (that is, a direct comparison of one thing with another introduced by "like," "as," or "so"). *Christ is head of the church.* Paul has already described in 4:15–16 the way in which Christ is the head of the church. He is head in that the rest of the body derives from him the health and strength that allows each part to play its own distinctive role. It is a headship of love, not of control; of nurture, not of suppression. The word "head" when used today has the sense of "ruler" or "authority." However, in Greek when "head" is used in a metaphorical sense as it is here, it means "origin" as in the "source (head) of a river." Woman has her origins in man (Gen. 2:18–23) just as the church has its origins in Christ. *the Savior.* The emphasis in this analogy is not on Christ as Lord, but on Christ as Savior. Paul is not saying that husbands are to express "headship" through the exertion of some sort of authority (as befits a "lord"), but through the expression of sacrificial love (as characterized by the Savior).

5:25 *love your wives.* This is the main thing Paul says to husbands. It is so important that he repeats this injunction three times (vv. 25,28,33). As for Greek culture, although cer-

tain philosophers such as Aristotle taught that men ought to love their wives, they used a mild word for love (*phileo*) signifying the sort of affection a person has for family. Here, however, Paul urges a far stronger type of love: *agape*, which is characterized by sacrificial, self-giving action. *just as also Christ loved the church and gave Himself for her.* Paul now makes quite clear in what sense he is speaking of Christ as head over the church. Two actions characterize Christ's role for the church: love and sacrifice. The husband is called upon to act toward his wife in the same way—that is, to die for her. (This is how Christ "gave himself up for the church.") A wife is asked to "submit" not to "authority," but to "sacrificial love."

5:25–27 In comparing the marriage relationship to the relationship between Christ and the church, Paul is following a long tradition in Scripture. The Old Testament often pictured God's relationship to his people in terms of a marriage covenant (Isa. 54:4–6; Jer. 2:1–3; 31:31–32). In the New Testament, Christ is seen as the bridegroom (Mark 2:19–20; John 3:29).

5:26 *the washing of water.* The reference is to the bridal bath prior to the wedding that was the custom of both Jews and Greeks. The action in view here is Christian baptism. *by the word.* This refers either to the confession of faith by the baptismal candidate, or more likely to the cleansing affect the Word of God has on the believer.

5:27 *to present the church.* At a Jewish wedding, the bride was presented to the groom by a friend. This was understood as a sacred duty, because God first performed it when he brought Eve to Adam (Gen. 2:22). In this case, Jesus is both he who presents and he who receives the bride. *splendor.* On one level, this word refers to the beautiful garments worn by the bride. On another level, it refers to the very radiance of God himself. The church, his bride, has about her the aura of God (as did Moses when he came off Mount Sinai—Ex. 34:29–35), a gift given her by the bridegroom. *without spot or wrinkle.* The bridegroom has removed any trace of disease (pox marks or leprosy), disfigurement or neglect.

5:28–31 In describing how husbands are to love their wives, Paul turns from the rather exalted vision of Christ's love for the church to the more mundane (but entirely realistic) level of the husband's love for himself!

5:28 *their own bodies.* The deep-rooted instinct to care for and protect oneself is to be carried over to the wife (who, through sexual intercourse, has become one flesh with her husband).

5:31 *one flesh.* Paul does not view marriage as some sort of spiritual covenant devoid of sexuality. His second illustration of how a husband is to love his wife (vv. 28–31) revolves around their sexual union, as is made explicit here by his quotation of Genesis 2:24.

5:33 *love his wife as himself.* In Leviticus 19:18, the Israelites are called upon to "love your neighbor as yourself." The gauge by which husbands will know if they are, indeed, loving their wives properly is self-love: "Is this how I want to be loved?" Husbands, according to Paul, can use this same gauge for measuring their love for their wives.

Authority

Scripture Ephesians 6:1–9

> **LAST WEEK** *Marriage was our topic in last week's session, as we looked at the roles of both husband and wife. Paul challenged us with some very controversial commands that are countercultural in today's world. Marriage was also used as an example of Christ's love for the church and we were reminded of how we need to submit to Jesus in every area of our life. This week we will focus on how to follow Christ in roles where we are in authority as well as under authority.*

 Ice-Breaker Connect With Your Group (15 minutes)

Growing up can be fun, and it can be not so fun. Surprisingly, jobs are the same way! Take turns sharing some of your unique life experiences with growing up and with working.

Leader
Open with a word of prayer, and then introduce any new people or visitors. Select one, two or all three Ice-Breaker questions to begin the study.

1. Who were you most like in your childhood behavior?

   ○ Michael Jackson.
   ○ Marie Osmond.
   ○ Charlie Brown.
   ○ Tiger Woods
   ○ Dennis the Menace.
   ○ Other _____.

2. Are you, or will you be, more strict or more lenient with your own kids than your parents were with you? Or about the same?

3. Have you ever held a job or other responsibility that felt like slavery?

Bible Study Read Scripture and Discuss (30 minutes)

Matters of the Christian home are not limited to husbands and wives, but also involve children and parents. Paul even carries the theme of unity into the workplace, addressing the way in which slaves and masters are to treat one another within the body of Christ. Read Ephesians 6:1–9 and note how in every relationship we are to follow the Lord's command of love.

Leader
Ask two group members, selected ahead of time, to read aloud the Scripture passage. Then discuss the Questions for Interaction, dividing into subgroups of three to six.

Authority

Reader One: 6 Children, obey your parents in the Lord, because this is right. ²Honor your father and mother—which is the first commandment with a promise— ³that it may go well with you and that you may have a long life in the land.

Reader Two: ⁴And fathers, don't stir up anger in your children, but bring them up in the training and instruction of the Lord.

Reader One: ⁵Slaves, obey your human masters with fear and trembling, in the sincerity of your heart, as to Christ. ⁶Don't work only while being watched, in order to please men, but as slaves of Christ, do God's will from your heart. ⁷Render service with a good attitude, as to the Lord and not to men, ⁸knowing that whatever good each one does, slave or free, he will receive this back from the Lord.

Reader Two: ⁹And masters, treat them the same way, without threatening them, because you know that both their and your Master is in heaven, and there is no favoritism with Him.

Ephesians 6:1–9

Questions for Interaction

Leader
Refer to the Summary and Study Notes at the end of this session as needed. If 30 minutes is not enough time to answer all of the questions in this section, conclude the Bible Study by answering question 7.

1. What do you usually do on Mother's Day or Father's Day to honor your parents?

    ○ Send flowers.
    ○ Give them a call.
    ○ Send a card saying how much I appreciate them.
    ○ Pray for them.
    ○ Other _____.

2. Why should children obey their parents? How long are children to obey their parents?

3. In what ways might fathers "stir up anger" (v. 4) in their children?

4. How does a father bring up his children "in the training and instruction of the Lord"?

5. What is required of a godly employee? A godly employer?

6. On a scale of 1 (halfheartedly) to 10 (wholeheartedly), how enthusiastic have you been about serving the Lord through your work lately?

7. What is God saying to you in this passage about your family or work situation?

Going Deeper   If your group has time and/or wants a challenge, go on to this question.

8. In verse 4, why does Paul single out fathers instead of parents? What if the mother is a Christian and the father is not?

 Caring Time Apply the Lesson and Pray for One Another (15 minutes)

Nobody ever has a perfect childhood, and nobody makes a perfect parent. Very few of us ever find perfect jobs, either. This group can be a good source of support, encouragement and advice on such topics. Take some time to share together and support one another in prayer.

Leader
Following the Caring Time, discuss with your group how they would like to celebrate the last session next week. Also, discuss the possibility of splitting into two groups or continuing together with another study.

1. What is something you did this last week to help you grow in your faith? What is something you can do in the coming week?

2. How can the group pray for your work situation?

3. How can the group support you in your role as parent or child?

NEXT WEEK *Today we examined the proper roles for those in authority and those under authority. We were reminded that we should honor our parents and our children. We were also told to do our work for Christ and his glory. During the coming week, ask the Lord to show you how to do well in both roles, both at work and at home. Next week we will learn how to arm ourselves for the true conflict that rages around us, the conflict against the enemy of our souls.*

Summary: Paul continues his discussion of the three basic sets of relationships that dominate most people's lives. Here he deals with relationships within a family (between parents and children), and the relationship between slaves and masters. Paul begins by urging children to "obey," and then gives four reasons for such obedience: (1) they are "in the Lord"; (2) it is the "right" thing to do; (3) God commands obedience; and (4) obedience brings a rich reward. Parents are then urged to limit the exercise of their authority, and to train their children in the ways of the Lord. To slaves Paul says, "render service with a good attitude." Then he says to masters, "treat them in the same way."

6:1–3 Paul does not simply command obedience on the part of children. He gives reasons for it. In other words, Paul does not take obedience for granted. In the same way that he addressed husbands and wives (and gave each a rationale for their behavior), he also does the same for children.

6:1 *Children.* The very fact that Paul even addresses children is remarkable. Normally, all such instructions would come through their parents. That he addresses children in this public letter means that children were in attendance with their families at worship when such a letter would have been read. Paul does not define a "child" here; i.e., he does not deal with the question of when a child becomes an adult, and thus ceases to be under parental authority. This is not a real problem, however, since each culture has its own definition of when adulthood begins. Even as adults, though, children are expected to "honor" their parents. *obey.* Paul tells the children to "obey" ("follow," "be subject to," literally, "listen to"). He uses a different word from the one used when speaking of the relationship between wives and husbands. Although "obey" is a stronger word than "submit," it is not without limits. *in the Lord.* This is the first reason children are to obey their parents. There are two ways in which this phrase can be taken: Obey your parents because you are a Christian, and/or obey your parents in everything that is compatible with your commitment to Christ. *because this is right.* This is

the second of four reasons Paul gives for obedience. "Children obey parents. That is simply the way it is," Paul says. It is not confined to Christian ethics; it is standard behavior in any society.

6:2 *"Honor your father and mother."* Paul begins to quote the fifth commandment. This is the third reason children should obey parents. God commands it. *the first commandment with a promise.* Paul probably means "first in importance," since the second commandment (Ex. 20:4–6) promises God's love to those who love God.

6:3 This is the fourth reason for obedience. It produces good rewards. Here, Paul identifies the two aspects of the promise. It involved material well-being and long life. The promise is probably not only for individual children, but also for the emotional health of the community of which they are a part.

6:4 Just as children have a duty to obey, parents have the duty to instruct children with gentleness and restraint. *fathers.* The model for a father is that of God, the "Father of all" (4:6). This view of fatherhood stands in sharp contrast to the harsh Roman father, who had the power of life and death over his children. *stir up anger.* Parents are to be responsible for not provoking hostility on the part of their children. By humiliating children, being cruel to them, over-indulging them, or being unreasonable, parents squash children (rather than encourage them). *bring them up.* This verb is literally, "nourish" or "feed" them. *training.* This word can be translated "discipline." *instruction.* The emphasis here is on what is said verbally to children.

6:5–8 That Paul should even address slaves is amazing. In the first century, they were often considered more akin to farm animals than free citizens. Slaves were "living tools" according to Aristotle. Yet Paul speaks to them as people able to choose and to decide—quite revolutionary for his era.

6:5 *obey.* Paul is not counseling rebellion (an impossibility in any case, given the conditions of the first century, and a cause which could lead only to massive bloodshed). He tells slaves to "obey" and to do so "with fear and trembling." He tells them to "render service." (v.7) The word "obey" is the same one that Paul used to define the child's duty to the parent. *human.* As opposed to "heavenly." Paul reminds slaves that although they may be "owned" by another human being at the moment, ultimately they belong to Christ, who is their true Lord. *sincerity of your heart.* Or "with singleness of heart." Paul calls for service to be given with integrity. Slaves are to give their masters the same wholehearted devotion they would give to the Lord. *Christ.* In each of the four verses addressed to slaves, Christ is mentioned.

6:6 *while being watched.* This is a good rendering of the phrase that reads literally, "not by way of eye-service as men-pleasers." In other words, don't just pretend to be serving wholeheartedly when, in fact, you only work when you are watched (and then simply to gain favor with your master).

6:7 When work is done for the Lord as part of obedience to him, it takes on a whole new character.

6:8 *receive this back.* The life of many slaves was hard and bleak, and there was little hope that it would change. In this context, the hope of future reward was not trivial, but of central importance.

6:9 *treat them the same way.* Paul applies the golden rule to slave owners: to get service and respect, give it to slaves. This was a revolutionary concept. This was the way of mutual submission for slave and master; i.e., mutual respect. *without threatening them.* In the same way that parents are not to exasperate children, masters are not to browbeat slaves. Punishment was the usual way of controlling slaves. Paul says, "Don't even use threats against the powerless." *no favoritism.* The seeds of emancipation are sown here. Paul is pointing out the basic equality between slave and master in the sight of God (see also v. 8).

The Armor of God

Scripture Ephesians 6:10–24

LAST WEEK *In last week's session, we continued to focus on relationships and how we should treat one another with honor and respect. Children are to honor and obey their parents and employees are to respect their employers and work for Christ and his glory. This week we will learn how to arm ourselves against the enemy of our souls.*

Ice-Breaker Connect With Your Group (15 minutes)

If you were in a real battle, you'd probably feel pretty vulnerable and helpless if you didn't have any weapons. However, life can feel like that sometimes. Take turns sharing your thoughts and experiences about armed conflict.

Leader
Begin this final session with a word of prayer and thanksgiving for this time together. Select from the following Ice-Breaker questions to begin the study.

1. What is your favorite movie, book or story about combat?

    - ○ *The Three Musketeers.*
    - ○ *Monty Python and the Holy Grail.*
    - ○ *Lord of the Rings.*
    - ○ *Patton.*
    - ○ *Men in Tights.*
    - ○ Other _____.

2. Whom do you know that served in the military during a time of conflict? Did he or she see any action?

3. Can you name a person who has prayed for you faithfully over a period of years and helped you in your spiritual warfare?

Bible Study Read Scripture and Discuss (30 minutes)

Paul concludes his book with some essential teaching on how a Christian is to find the capacity to imitate God, to walk in the light and to maintain unity by using the spiritual armor of God himself. Using an analogy of the armor and weaponry used by Roman soldiers, Paul explains that every Christian has a complete set of spiritual armor with which to fight against the Devil and his allies. Read Ephesians 6:10–24 and note the importance of prayer in spiritual warfare.

Leader
Select two group members ahead of time to read aloud the Scripture passage. Have one person read verses 10–17; and the other read verses 18–24. Then discuss the Questions for Interaction, dividing into subgroups of three to six.

The Armor of God

Reader One: [10]Finally, be strengthened by the Lord and by His vast strength. [11]Put on the full armor of God so that you can stand against the tactics of the Devil. [12]For our battle is not against flesh and blood, but against the rulers, against the authorities, against the world powers of this darkness, against the spiritual forces of evil in the heavens. [13]This is why you must take up the full armor of God, so that you may be able to resist in the evil day, and having prepared everything, to take your stand. [14]Stand, therefore,

with truth like a belt around your waist,

righteousness like armor on your chest,

[15]and your feet sandaled with readiness for the gospel of peace.

[16]In every situation take the shield of faith,

and with it you will be able to extinguish

the flaming arrows of the evil one.

[17]Take the helmet of salvation,

and the sword of the Spirit, which is God's word.

Reader Two: [18]With every prayer and request, pray at all times in the Spirit, and stay alert in this, with all perseverance and intercession for all the saints. [19]Pray also for me, that the message may be given to me when I open my mouth to make known with boldness the mystery of the gospel. [20]For this I am an ambassador in chains. Pray that I might be bold enough in Him to speak as I should.

[21]Tychicus, our dearly loved brother and faithful servant in the Lord, will tell you everything so that you also may know how I am and what I'm doing. [22]I am sending him to you for this very reason, to let you know how we are and to encourage your hearts.

[23]Peace to the brothers, and love with faith, from God the Father and the Lord Jesus Christ. [24]Grace be with all who have undying love for our Lord Jesus Christ.

Ephesians 6:10–24

Questions for Interaction

Leader
Refer to the Summary and Study Notes at the end of this session as needed. If 30 minutes is not enough time to answer all the questions in this section, conclude the Bible Study by answering question 7.

1. Where do you see the "tactics of the Devil" (v. 11) being played out in the world today?

   ○ In the media.
   ○ In the drug culture.
   ○ In racism.
   ○ In religious wars.
   ○ In the quest for wealth.
   ○ Other _____.
   Where do you see the "tactics of the Devil" in your own life?

2. How does Paul describe the enemy we face (v. 12)? How is that enemy to be defeated?

3. Roman soldiers would use a belt to keep their tunics from entangling their legs or arms. Why does Paul choose this as his metaphor for truth?

4. Why is righteousness like a breastplate of armor? What exactly does Paul mean by "righteousness" (v. 14)?

5. Why is the Gospel pictured as sandals? What might this mean for the future of our group?

6. What principles does Paul give for how a Christian should pray (vv. 18–20)? How important is prayer in your life, and how do you use it to defeat the enemy?

7. What have you been struggling against lately? How does this passage help equip you?

Going Deeper   If your group has time and/or wants a challenge, go on to this question.

8. Why is faith a shield while God's word is a sword? What can we do to make our Bible study more meaningful so it becomes an effective weapon against the enemy?

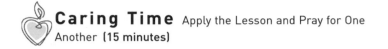

Caring Time Apply the Lesson and Pray for One Another (15 minutes)

Gather around each other now in this final time of sharing and prayer. Encourage one another to have faith and hope and to put on the "armor of God" as you go back out into the world.

1. On a scale of 1 (baby steps) to 10 (giant leaps), how has your relationship with God progressed over the last 12 weeks?

2. What lessons have been the most important or significant to you in this study?

3. How can we as friends continue to support and love one another in the coming weeks?

Notes on Ephesians 6:10–24

Summary: Paul ends his letter where he began it: with a vision of the heavenly realms. However, unlike chapter one, where his focus was on God's kingdom, this time his focus is on Satan's realm. In chapter one, he was looking ahead to the treasures laid up in heaven for God's children. Here he explains that, prior to that glorious day, the children of God must wrestle with evil principalities and powers.

6:10 *be strengthened ... by His vast strength.* Paul uses the same three words here as he used in 1:19, when he first described God's incomparable power. In order to wage successful warfare against Satan, the Christian must draw upon God's own power. This is a power outside us from beyond. This is not a natural power generated by the Christian.

6:11–12 Paul defines the Christian's opponent in this spiritual warfare. He is crafty ("the tactics of the Devil"). He is powerful ("the world powers of this darkness"). And he is wicked ("the spiritual forces of evil"). In other words, the Devil is a real opponent, and his legions are not to be taken lightly.

6:11 *Put on.* It is not enough simply to rely passively on God's power. The Christian must do something. Specifically, he or she must "put on"

God's armor. *full armor.* Paul uses here the term *panoplia* (from which the English word "panoply" comes), which can be understood as the complete catalog of equipment needed by a soldier. *so that you can stand against.* God's armor enables the Christian to stand against Satan. *the tactics of the Devil.* Evil does not operate in the light. It lurks in shadows and strikes unexpectedly, with cleverness and subtlety.

6:12 *our battle.* The King James Version translates this phrase as "we wrestle" and indeed Paul shifts his analogy here from the military field to the gymnasium and an athletic contest. *flesh and blood.* Human beings. *rulers/authorities/ powers/spiritual forces.* By these various titles, Paul names the diverse spiritual forces that rage against humanity. These are intangible spiritual entities whose will is often worked out through concrete historical, economic, political, social and institutional structures. Part of the call to Christians is to identify the places where these evil powers are at work. *the world powers of this darkness.* This phrase can be translated as "the world rulers of this darkness." *forces of evil.* Another characteristic of these supernatural beings is wickedness. They are of the darkness, not of the light.

6:13 *the evil day.* Although Paul may have in mind the final Day of Judgment when Christ returns and the hostile powers are subdued once and for all, the immediate reference is to those special times of pressure and testing that come to all Christians, at which point steadfast resistance of evil is called for and made possible by the full armor of God. *take your stand.* This is the second time Paul has spoken about "standing fast" (v. 11). Twice more, he will urge the same thing (vv. 13–14). This is the basic posture of the Christian in the face of evil: resistance. "Standing firm" is a military image. Paul may well have in mind the fighting position of the Roman legions. Fully equipped soldiers were virtually invulnerable to enemy onslaught— unless they panicked and broke ranks. As long as they "stood firm" when the enemy attacked, they would prevail in the long run. Most of all their equipment, as will be seen in verses 14–17, was designed to enable them to "hold the position." This is key to resisting evil.

6:14–17 Paul describes six pieces of armor in roughly the order in which a Roman soldier would put them on in preparation for battle. All the pieces of armor (except one) are defensive in nature, rather than aggressive in intent. Each piece of armor is used by Paul as a metaphor for what the Christian needs in order to stand against the dark forces.

6:14 *truth like a belt.* The leather belt on which the Roman soldier hung his sword, and by which he secured his tunic and armor (so he would be unimpeded in battle). The "truth" referred to is the inner integrity and sincerity by which the Christian fights evil. Lying and deceit are tactics of the enemy. *righteousness like armor on your chest.* The breastplate (or "mail") was the major piece of armor for the Roman soldier. Made of metal and leather, it protected his vital organs. "Righteousness" refers to the right standing before God that is the status of the Christian, out of which moral conduct and character emerges. In the battle against evil, it is vital to have an assured relationship with God as well as the kind of character that stands in sharp contrast to the evil that is being resisted.

6:15 *feet sandaled.* These are the leather half boots worn by the Roman legionnaire, with heavy studded soles that enabled him to dig in and resist being pushed out of place. *readiness.* This term can be translated as "firmness" or "steadfastness," in which case the "gospel of peace" is understood to provide the solid foundation on which the Christian stands in the fight against evil.

6:16 *the shield of faith.* A large, oblong shield constructed of layers of wood on an iron frame, which was then covered with linen and hide. When wet, such a shield could absorb "flaming arrows." *flaming arrows.* These were pitch-soaked arrows. Their aim was not so much to kill a soldier, as to set him aflame and cause him to break rank and create panic.

6:17 *the helmet of salvation.* A heavy, metal head covering lined with felt and sponge, which gave substantial protection to the soldier's head from all but the heaviest ax blow. The sure knowledge that one's salvation is secure—that the outcome of the battle is already known—is the final defense against Satan. *sword.* A short, stabbing sword used for personal combat. The sword is the only piece of offensive equipment in the armor.

6:18 *pray.* Paul does not consider prayer a seventh weapon. Rather, it underlies the whole process of spiritual warfare. *in the Spirit.* The Bible, the Word of God, is the sword of the Spirit. So, too, the Spirit guides prayer.

6:21–24 It now remains for Paul to say good-bye. His letter is complete. He has said all that is necessary about the new reality created by God (the multinational church) and the new style of life that its members are to live out. The last four verses are more "housekeeping" in nature than content-oriented. Paul has two things to say in these verses. First, he commends Tychicus and indicates that he will convey information to them about his state of affairs. Second, he concludes the letter with the traditional Greek "wish for blessing," though in a nonn-traditional, Christianized fashion. In fact, by his choice of benediction, he sums up the whole book. The two key words here are "grace" and "peace." No two words could summarize the message of the letter more succinctly.

6:22 *encourage.* Paul worries about them, and wants to reassure them and encourage their faith. Yet it is Paul who is in prison facing trial and who, by all accounts, should be the one receiving the encouragement!

6:23 *Peace.* This has been a major theme of his letter. This peace between people became possible when Jesus made peace between God and humanity (by reconciling men and women to God through the Cross). Jesus' message was a message of peace (2:14–18). *love.* Likewise, love has been a major theme in Ephesians (1:4–5; 2:4–5; 4:2,15–16; 5:1–2,22–33).

6:24 *Grace.* Paul's third request is that they continue to receive God's grace. Grace, too, has been a theme in Ephesians. It is by grace that we have been saved (1:6–7; 2:5–8); it was by grace that Paul was called into ministry (3:7); and it is by grace that each Christian has received gifts of ministry (4:7).

Individual and Group Needs Survey

Check the types of studies that you find most interesting:

❏ Issues about spiritual development, such as learning to love like God does or knowing God's will.

❏ Studying about the life and message of Jesus Christ.

❏ Issues about personal development, such as managing stress or understanding the stages of growth in marriage.

❏ Learning about the major truths of the Christian faith.

❏ Studying the teaching of the Apostle Paul.

❏ Working through specific areas of personal struggle, such as coping with teenagers or recovering from divorce.

❏ Learning about the books of the New Testament other than the Gospels and Epistles of Paul.

Rank the following factor in order of importance to you with 1 being the highest and five being the lowest:

_____ The passage of Scripture that is being studied.

_____ The topic or issue that is being discussed.

_____ The affinity of group members (age, vocation, interest).

_____ The mission of the group (service projects, evangelism, starting groups).

_____ Personal encouragement.

Rank the following spiritual development needs in order of interest to you with 1 being the highest and 5 being the lowest:

_____ Learning how to become a follower of Christ.

_____ Gaining a basic understanding of the truths of the faith.

_____ Improving my disciplines of devotion, prayer, reading Scripture.

_____ Gaining a better knowledge of what is in the Bible.

_____ Applying the truths of Scripture to my life.

Of the various studies listed below check the appropriate boxes to indicate:

P - if you would be interested in studying this for your **personal needs**

G - if you think it would be helpful for your **group**

F - if **friends** that are not in the group would come to a group studying this subject

Growing in Christ Series (7-week studies)	P	G	F
Keeping Your Cool: Dealing with Stress	❏	❏	❏
Personal Audit: Assessing Your life	❏	❏	❏
Seasons of Growth: Stages of Marriage	❏	❏	❏
Setting Your Moral Compass: Personal Morals	❏	❏	❏
Women of Faith (8 weeks)	❏	❏	❏
Men of Faith	❏	❏	❏
Being Single and the Spiritual Quest	❏	❏	❏

Foundations of the Faith (7-week studies)   P   G   F

	P	G	F
Knowing Jesus	❑	❑	❑
Foundational Truths	❑	❑	❑
God and the Journey to Truth	❑	❑	❑
The Christian in the Postmodern World	❑	❑	❑

Fellowship Church Series (6-week studies)

	P	G	F
Wired for Worship (worship as a lifestyle)	❑	❑	❑
X-Trials: Takin' Life to the X-treme (James)	❑	❑	❑
Virtuous Reality: The Relationships of David	❑	❑	❑
Praying for Keeps (life of prayer)	❑	❑	❑
Character Tour (developing godly character)	❑	❑	❑

Becoming a Disciple (7-week studies)

	P	G	F
Discovering God's Will	❑	❑	❑
Time for a Checkup	❑	❑	❑
Learning to Love	❑	❑	❑
Making Great Kids	❑	❑	❑
Becoming Small-Group Leaders	❑	❑	❑

Understanding the Savior (13-week studies)

	P	G	F
Jesus, the Early Years (Mark 1 – 8)	❑	❑	❑
Jesus, the Final Days (Mark 9 – 16)	❑	❑	❑
John: God in the Flesh (John 1 – 11)	❑	❑	❑
John: The Passion of the Son (John 12 – 21)	❑	❑	❑
The Life of Christ	❑	❑	❑
Jesus, the Teacher: Sermon on the Mount	❑	❑	❑
The Parables of Jesus	❑	❑	❑
The Miracles of Jesus	❑	❑	❑

The Message of Paul

	P	G	F
Who We Really Are: Romans 1 – 7 (13 weeks)	❑	❑	❑
Being a Part of God's Plan: Romans 8 – 16 (13 weeks)	❑	❑	❑
Taking on Tough Issues: 1 Corinthians (13 weeks)	❑	❑	❑
Living by Grace: Galatians (13 weeks)	❑	❑	❑
Together in Christ: Ephesians (12 weeks)	❑	❑	❑
Running the Race: Philippians (7 weeks)	❑	❑	❑
Passing the Torch: 1 & 2 Timothy (13 weeks)	❑	❑	❑

Men of Purpose Series (13-week studies geared to men)

	P	G	F
Overcoming Adversity: Insights into the Life of Joseph	❑	❑	❑
Fearless Leadership: Insights into the Life of Joshua	❑	❑	❑
Unwavering Tenacity: Insights into the Life of Elijah	❑	❑	❑
Shoulder to Shoulder: Insights into the Life of the Apostles	❑	❑	❑

Words of Faith

	P	G	F
The Church on Fire: Acts 1 – 14 (13 weeks)	❑	❑	❑
An Irrepressible Witness: Acts 15 – 28 (13 weeks)	❑	❑	❑
The True Messiah: Hebrews (13 weeks)	❑	❑	❑
Faith at Work: James (12 weeks)	❑	❑	❑
Staying the Course: 1 Peter (10 weeks)	❑	❑	❑
Walking in the Light: 1 John (11 weeks)	❑	❑	❑
The End of Time: Revelation 1 – 12 (13 weeks)	❑	❑	❑
The New Jerusalem: Revelation 13 – 22 (13 weeks)	❑	❑	❑

301 Bible Studies with Home Work Assignments (13-week studies)

	P	G	F
Life of Christ: Behold the Man	❑	❑	❑
Sermon on the Mount: Examining Your Life	❑	❑	❑
Parables: Virtual Reality	❑	❑	❑
Miracles: Signs and Wonders	❑	❑	❑
Ephesians: Our Riches in Christ	❑	❑	❑
Philippians: Joy under Stress	❑	❑	❑
James: Walking the Talk	❑	❑	❑
1 John: The Test of Faith	❑	❑	❑

Life Connections Series (Unique series blends master-teacher larger group format with effective small-group encounters; 13-week studies)

	P	G	F
Essential Truth: Knowing Christ Personally	❑	❑	❑
Vital Pursuits: Developing My Spiritual Life	❑	❑	❑
Authentic Relationships: Being Real in an Artificial World	❑	❑	❑
Unique Design: Connecting with the Christian Community	❑	❑	❑
Acts: Model for Today's Church	❑	❑	❑
Critical Decisions: Surviving in Today's World	❑	❑	❑
Colossians: Navigating Successfully Through Cultural Chaos	❑	❑	❑
Intentional Choices: Discovering Contentment in Stressful Times	❑	❑	❑
Unleashed Influence: Power of Servant Leadership	❑	❑	❑

Felt Need Series (7-week studies)

	P	G	F
Stress Management: Finding the Balance	❑	❑	❑
Healthy Relationships: Living Within Defined Boundaries	❑	❑	❑
Marriage Enrichment: Making a Good Marriage Better	❑	❑	❑

For the latest studies visit www.SerendipityHouse.com or call 1-800-525-9563.

Personal Notes

_____

_____

_____

_____

_____

_____

_____

_____

_____

_____

Personal Notes

Personal Notes